MW01282326

It's Already in Your Head

How Everything You Know About Caddyshack
Can Improve Your Mental Golf Game

by
Jared M. Wood

authorHOUSE™

1663 Liberty Drive, Suite 200
Bloomington, Indiana 47403
(800) 839-8640
www.AuthorHouse.com

This book is a work of fiction. People, places, events, and situations are the product of the author's imagination. Any resemblance to actual persons, living or dead, or historical events, is purely coincidental.

© 2005 Jared M. Wood. All Rights Reserved.

No part of this book may be reproduced, stored in a retrieval system, or transmitted by any means without the written permission of the author.

First published by AuthorHouse 06/07/05

ISBN: 1-4208-4345-1 (sc)

Library of Congress Control Number: 2005902630

Printed in the United States of America
Bloomington, Indiana

This book is printed on acid-free paper.

Caddyshack (1980) is copyrighted by Warner Bros.

To Celeste: Without your love and support, this would not have been possible.

To Mom: Without your love and support, nothing would have been possible.

To all my family and friends: You have helped me beyond measure and beyond what I can express in words. I appreciate all you've done and thank you for everything.

Table of Contents

Chapter 1: Buck Up, Buck

Young Buck swung out of his shoes, chunked a divot, and dribbled his last range ball to the 50-yard marker forty five degrees to his right. Disgusted, he whipped his club at his bag and shoved his hand in his pocket to scrounge for more range tokens. As he walked to the clubhouse, he heard Rich Daddy holler from down the range.

"Grip it and rip it, Young Buck!" Rich Daddy flashed a toothy grin from behind an expensive fortress of Titleist, Footjoy, and Nike. "That's my motto. Work's for me." As he swung his bag over his shoulder and headed for the first tee, he felt the need to add, "And Tiger!"

"Yeah, yeah," muttered Young Buck. "Fat Daddy and Tiger. I guess anyone can have a good swing if they pay enough for it."

Young Buck picked up his Super Bucket of 150 golf balls and winced. His hands throbbed with blisters, and his back ached. He was in no shape to go out and pound more golf balls, but he felt he couldn't quit now. He had a small money game on the weekend. He had to groove his swing, or his buddies would take all his money.

Walking back to his divot-infested perch on the range, Young Buck heard the unmistakable swoosh and click of a perfectly struck ball. He turned and saw Old Pearl standing at attention, watching the boring arc of his perfect shot.

Young Buck shook his head and asked himself how Pearl, a withered old man barely capable of carrying his bag, could strike such a beautiful ball. It didn't make any sense.

Buck tossed down his Super Bucket and began firing range balls every which way like a man possessed. Once, he shanked a ball off the hosel so badly that he almost hit the Old Pearl. Pearl didn't even notice.

When he had finished the bucket, Buck collapsed, worn out and frustrated. What was wrong with him? For months, he had desperately tried to groove a swing. He had practiced the swing he was taught by the club pro. He had done the drills and read the magazines. He had done everything he knew how to do and spent almost all of his meager funds. It was hopeless, he decided, and he contemplated quitting as he dragged his bag off the range.

"Quittin' so soon?" Pearl yelled at him.

"Maybe," Buck muttered to himself.

Buck pulled his last dollar bill out of his pocket, bought a bottled soda, and sat down on a bench near the range. It was a beautiful evening, and despite his horrid performance on the range, he felt the need to stick around, sit for a minute, and soak up the early evening air.

From his spot, he watched Pearl hitting balls. He noticed that he and Pearl did not practice the same way at all. While Buck gripped, ripped, and swung for the fences at a furious pace, Pearl was methodical. He worked a slower pace. His pile of balls was set a few feet away, requiring him to walk a few steps to retrieve his next ball to be struck. After placing his ball, he looked down the range for what seemed like a long time before he began to set up over the ball. When he set up, he was careful about his hands, feet, head, and shoulders. Every time he hit a ball, he went through the same routine: Retrieve a ball, set the ball, stare down the range, set up over the ball, glance down the range, waggle, swing. Every ball was better than Young Buck's best. Feeling disgusted again, Buck stood up and stomped toward the exit.

"Quittin' so soon?"

Buck quickly whirled around. He was startled to see Pearl staring at him from the range, his hand on his forehead like a makeshift sun visor.

"I can't play this game, I might as well quit!" Buck yelled.

Pearl shook his head. "Oh yeah?" Pearl said slowly and cheerfully with a benevolent smile on his face. "I wouldn't be so sure about that."

Now Buck was really mad. How could the old man be so cheery when it was so obvious that Buck was extremely irritated?

"What's the secret, old man?" Buck scowled, hoping to scare off the Pearl.

"No secret," said Pearl.

"If there's no secret, how can an old man like you be so much better than a Young Buck like me? Has to be a secret."

"No secret," repeated Old Pearl. "It's already in your head."

Buck snorted. "Yeah, I've heard that one before," he said sarcastically. "It's all in your head. Well I wish I knew what *it* was."

Pearl was amused with Young Buck's impatience and attitude. "*It*," Pearl said with emphasis, "*already is in your head.*" He pronounced each word carefully and slowly.

"Yeah, okay, old man. I get it. I have the power. I just need to believe in myself. I get it. Point taken. Thanks for the self-esteem lesson." Buck was half-smiling at the old man's trite lecture. This time he surely was leaving. He hoisted his bag over his shoulder and slowly shuffled away.

From the dwindling twilight filtering through the oaks onto the range, Buck heard Old Pearl say something quietly. It struck his attention, and maybe, a twinge of hope.

"Be back tomorrow at dawn for your first lesson."

Chapter 2: Pearl's Wisdom

Young Buck slept well that night. He had earned it through hours of work on the range. He dreamed of being on the range, hammering balls into oblivion like Fat Daddy and perfectly placing finessed shots like Old Pearl. In his sleep, he heard the words Old Pearl had said to him: "*It's already in your head. It's already in your head.*"

At first light, Young Buck awoke, renewed with energy. It was going to be a beautiful morning, he decided. He still wasn't sure what Old Pearl had in mind, but the old goat had promised a lesson that morning hadn't he? Maybe today would be the day for Buck's breakthrough.

Arriving at the range that morning, carrying his daily dose of Super Buckets, Buck noticed Old Pearl sitting on the bench waiting for him.

"Ready for your lesson, Young Buck?" the Pearl smiled.

"I think I am," Buck replied. "I have plenty of range balls for both of us."

Pearl laughed. "We don't need any balls today, Buck. Just brains," Pearl said poking a finger at Buck's cranium.

"I don't get it. How can we practice golf without any golf balls?" Buck mused.

"We're going to learn about the mental game of golf today," Pearl said with confidence.

"Oh. I was a little afraid you were going to say that," Buck admitted disappointedly. "I don't know if I am into that psychology stuff. I don't even have my swing grooved yet." Buck thought of Fat Rich Daddy and his powerful swing. "Besides, I don't want to do that sissy mental stuff. I want to grip it and rip it like Rich Daddy."

The old man smiled and put his hand on Young Buck's shoulder. "I understand, Buck. It can sound like a bunch of hocus pocus. But give me today to show you my method, and I think you'll be hooked. Deal?"

Buck looked at the old man. Somehow, in his confidence, Old Pearl suddenly looked much bigger, and in his doubt, Buck felt very small, shrunken. Reluctantly, he agreed to let Old Pearl give him one lesson.

"That a boy," Pearl crowed. "Now we're getting somewhere. Soon you'll be hitting balls like Rich Daddy and me."

"I don't know," Buck said sheepishly. "I don't have the money for expensive clubs and gadgets. I don't know if I will ever hit the ball like Rich Daddy."

"It's not expensive equipment that makes Rich Daddy such a good golfer," Pearl protested.

"It's not? What is it?"

"He had a good teacher."

"I already took lessons from Club Professional, and it didn't help," Buck said dejectedly.

"Not Club Pro," Pearl laughed. "Me! I was his teacher."

"You?" Buck said flabbergasted. "I never knew. You and Rich Daddy don't swing anything alike. You hit the ball well, but you don't hit it far like Rich Daddy. He grips it and…."

"Rips it. I know. But that is not what makes him a good golfer. Rich daddy is a good golfer because he has a strong mental game. And a strong mental game is the key to good golf."

"How so?" Buck asked.

"Whether one is a seasoned veteran of the links or has yet to pick up their first golf club, learning how to manage your thoughts on the course and range is extremely important. At the professional level, every player has a great swing, so players know that being in control of one's thoughts and emotions is the most important aspect of the game. Find a pro who doesn't have a specific plan for managing the game's mental component, and I'll show you a pro on the way to becoming an amateur."

Pearl continued, "At the amateur level, more emphasis is given to swing mechanics, but any amateur who has no knowledge of the mental game surely is not progressing at the optimum rate. From the pro to the outstanding amateur who has stalled in his or her progress to the person taking their first lesson, a good grasp of the mental game will make a great difference in one's ability to play the game well. It worked for Rich Daddy, and it will work for you. You already know everything you need to know. I just need to prove it to you."

"You keep saying that, but how do you know what I know? How can you possibly know that I can learn the mental game?" Buck demanded.

"I know because I have heard you and your friends."

"Heard us?" Buck said in surprise. "What did I say that was so smart about the mental game? I don't ever remember saying anything about it."

"You didn't know you were saying it at the time, but you said it, proving you know it. Buck, haven't I heard you 'Noonan!' your buddies over pressure filled putts to the delight of your Caddyshack-wise brethren?"

"Maybe," Buck said, frowning.

"And haven't you hauled off and hit a long one and heard one of your friends break into a quote about 'the Dalai Lama himself,' a big hitter in his own right?"

"Uh, yeah."

Pearl changed his voice to sound like Carl Spackler, the assistant greenskeeper in Caddyshack played by Bill Murray. "And Buck, didn't I once see you *whacking* nostalgic in the flower bed, muttering about the 'Cinderella story, about to become the Master's Champion'?"

Buck burst into laughter at the old man's imitation of the classic character. "Time out, Old Pearl," Young Buck said making a T with his hands. "Now I am really confused. Throw me a bone here."

"I'll do better than that. I can teach you valuable lessons by associating mental game principles with quotes and scenes from the movie Caddyshack," Pearl said proudly.

"Whoa! Hold it, old man. Are you telling me that all the movie lines I know are good for the mental game of golf? Everyone always tells me that's 'useless knowledge.' Now you are telling me that it is a gold mine of information?"

"That's what I'm saying. Are you interested now?" Pearl asked.

"I guess so. Tell me more."

Pearl began to teach his method. "Like many of the golfers I know, you have a considerable amount of your long-term memory storage locked up in golf movie quotes and scenes, and you regularly drop them on your playing partners. Perhaps, others have even ridiculed you for your savant-like recall of golf movie scenes, accused you of wasting brain space on such trivial facts, or lamented about the great things that go undone because of your inability to fill your head with any information of substance."

"Yeah. I guess it's not a flattering picture, but I have wasted a lot of time memorizing golf movie quotes," Buck admitted.

"Mmm," Pearl hummed. "An unflattering shoe to wear indeed, but if the shoe fits, I say, wear it. It is nothing of which to be ashamed."

"I still don't see how knowing so much about Caddyshack will help me learn the mental game and become a better golfer. It's just a movie, not real golf. It does seem a little useless."

Old Pearl expounded upon his theory. "The way I see things, it really isn't a problem if your head is full of useless knowledge about a movie based on maladjusted golfers and a mechanical gopher. There are worse things you could know. Actually, having a great knowledge of golf movies will greatly enhance your ability to learn the mental game."

"How does knowing movie quotes help someone learn about the mental game of golf?" Buck queried thoughtfully.

"Having knowledge of any subject allows you to learn related knowledge quickly by associating new ideas with the information already stored in you memory," Pearl explained. "It's like having a pre-installed hook on which to hang something. You simply attach new knowledge to old."

"I think I get it," Buck said. "You are going to take a quote I already know, and make it into a lesson on the mental game. That way, all I have to do is think of a quote I already know, and I will automatically remember the mental game lesson that goes with it."

"You catch on pretty quick, Buck."

"Great. Let's go to the range. I'm ready for my first lesson," Buck called as he ran for the door.

7

"Wait!" Pearl shouted. "Have a little patience, Buck. We can start right now, but first, we need to do a little filmwork. Follow me to the clubhouse lounge."

Chapter 3: Be the Ball

Filmwork

Buck settled into one of the comfortable chairs in the lounge while Pearl cued up a DVD to show on the television. A scene from Caddyshack appeared on the screen.

The Scene: It is a resplendent morning at Bushwood Country Club. Member Ty Webb is golfing with his caddy, Danny Noonan. Through their conversation we learn that Danny is anxious and confused over his choice of future careers and is seeking input from others. A preference test Danny took indicated that he should become a "firewatcher." Not quite knowing how to prepare for a career in the inferno supervising arts, Danny seeks Ty's advice. After advising Danny that doing drugs everyday is good and working at a lumberyard is a fine job (Ty owns several lumberyards, though he is unsure of their locations), Ty attempts to impart some salutary advice to Danny.

The Quote: Ty to Danny: "I'm gonna give you a little advice. There's a force in the universe that makes things happen. All you have to do is get in touch with it. Stop thinking. Let things happen. And be the ball."

> ### The Lesson: Focus on a Target
> *To play the best golf of which we are capable, we must learn to unify our body and mind. To do this, we must focus intently on a specific target - the spot to which we want to hit the ball. This mental focus sends a clear signal to our body, telling it exactly what we want it to do.*

Out on the range, Pearl began his instruction. "Tee one up," he said to Buck.

"You want me to hit one? I thought we were going to learn about the mental game."

"We are. But I want you to hit one first."

"OK. What should I think about when I am hitting?" Buck asked as he set up over his ball, proud of himself for realizing their purpose for the lesson.

"Nothing," Pearl responded.

Buck halted his practice swing and turned to face Pearl. "Nothing?"

Pearl nodded quickly then shook his head. "Nothing," he repeated.

Buck was confused. "I thought you were going to teach me about the mental game. You know, *thinking!* Now you are telling me to think about nothing?"

Pearl just shrugged and smiled.

Buck was a bit annoyed with the old man's first lesson, but trying to be a good student, he placed a tee in the ground and set a ball on top of it. He took a few practice swings, trying to think of nothing in particular. *"Nothing, Nothing,"* he kept thinking to himself. After a few more practice swings, he stepped up to the ball and swung, thinking about thinking about nothing. He hit the ball hard, but it was a worm-burner that scorched the ground and ended up in the left rough. Buck shook his head and looked back at Pearl, who was smiling.

"Well that didn't work, Pearl. This is great," he said sarcastically. "My first mental game lesson and all you've done is smile and tell me to think about nothing." Buck was fuming. He expected instant progress.

"And?" Pearl started, waiting for a response.

"And what? You saw how I hit the ball. Your advice wasn't any help."

"What were you thinking about when you hit the ball?" Pearl asked.

"I was thinking about nothing. Like you said."

"Mmm," Pearl nodded. "What were you really thinking about? Be honest. It is very important that you are honest about your thoughts, or I won't know how to help you."

Buck blew out a deep breath. *Give the old man a chance* he thought to himself. "Okay. I was really thinking about how stupid it is that you told me to think about nothing. How in the world can you think about nothing? I mean, it's basically impossible to think about nothing."

"It is a difficult thing to do," Pearl admitted. "That is one reason why so many people are lousy golfers. They cannot train themselves to think the way they need to think to play good golf."

"But Pearl, there has to be more to the mental game than thinking about nothing. What is your point? Will you just give me the lesson you promised?" Buck pleaded.

Pearl laughed. "We've already begun our lesson, Buck."

"Huh?"

"What did we learn in our filmwork today, Buck? Think now. Ty gives Danny some advice in that scene. What advice did he give him?"

Buck thought hard. He replayed the scene in his mind until he came up with the answer. "He said, 'Be the ball'?"

"Actually, Ty's exact words to Danny were: 'I'm gonna give you a little advice. There's a force in the universe that makes things happen. All you have to do is get in touch with it. Stop thinking. Let things happen. And be the ball.' Sound familiar?"

"Yeah, it does," Buck admitted. "He said to stop thinking. Like you told me to think of nothing."

"Mmmhmm. And be the ball." Pearl made a temple with his two index fingers and put them to his lips. He paused to let his words sink into Buck's cranium. "I want you to try something, Buck. Have an open mind please."

"Okay, I'll try. But you know I'm not really into this thinking and feeling stuff."

Pearl continued despite Buck's meager protests. "I want you to close your eyes and take a few deep breaths."

Buck glared at Pearl for a second, hoping to coax the old man into letting him out of this exercise. Pearl was solid, though. He didn't flinch. Buck gave up and closed his eyes.

"Good. Take a few deep breaths, drawing attention to the rise and fall of your breath. If your mind wanders, simply bring your attention back to your breath. Clear your mind of all distractions."

Pearl observed Buck's slight physical movements. When he saw Buck's facial and shoulder muscles relax, he said, "That's good. Just relax." He watched Buck take a few more deep breaths. In a soft, deep voice he instructed, "Now, picture yourself being the ball. Not you imagining yourself being the ball, actually picture yourself as a dimpled, surlyn covered, bleach white balata sitting up high on a tee, about to be whaled on by Ty Webb. What thoughts do you have? What are you thinking as you're being the ball?"

Buck tried his best to follow the old man's request. He thought as hard as he ever had thought before. He could see himself as a golf ball with his own face. But try as he might, he couldn't come up with an answer to the old man's question. He couldn't figure out what a golf ball would think.

Pearl could sense the mental effort the young man was putting into this exercise. Buck's eyes were closed tightly, his face contorted from the effort of such deep thought. Pearl was pleased and comically amused at his student's attempt to picture himself thinking like a golf ball. He decided to let the kid off the hook.

He leaned in close to Buck's ear and shouted, "Nothing!"

Buck was startled. He looked wide-eyed at Pearl.

Pearl reiterated, "Nothing! That's what you're thinking! You're a golf ball for Bishop Pickering's sake. You don't have any thoughts!"

Buck continued to display the deer-in-the-headlights look.

"At the most, I'll allow you a level of personification affording you an awareness of where you are resting, your lie, and where you are going, your target. But for the love of Lacy Underall, you have no thoughts, my fair-weather friend of the fairway."

Buck suddenly got the joke and started laughing. He knew the old man had fooled him, and he was more than a little relieved that Pearl wasn't serious about making him think as a golf ball thinks.

Pearl explained further. "And as the golf ball thinks, so should you aspire to think. As you stand over the ball and go through a preshot routine, which we will discuss later, you should gradually pare down your thoughts until you are only aware of a laser-like focus on your target. At that point, you are the intellectual equivalent of a Maxfli. You are the ball, and you may go ahead and swing."

Buck thought about this information for a moment. "So you really aren't telling me not to think," he deduced. "You are really telling me only to think about my target."

"Pretty much," Pearl said. "You should be focused on a mental picture of your target, but you shouldn't be actively thinking about anything. Just focus on your target, and let your muscles make the swing without too much interference from your thoughts."

Buck looked perplexed. "Why does it work, Pearl?"

Pearl explained. "Although part of Ty's point is rooted in his own Zen philosophy, part of it is dead on with scientific research in sport and cognitive psychology. If we change the part about 'a force in the universe' to 'a unity between your mind and body,' Ty's quote describes the essence of what we want to do as we set up over the golf ball. In essence, he is saying there is a unity between your mind and body that makes things happen. 'All you have to do is get in touch with it. Stop thinking. Let things happen. And be the ball.'"

"A unity between the mind and body, Pearl?"

"Hundreds of years ago, philosophers thought that the mind and body were separate entities in form and function. This school of thought, known as dualism, was replaced as more information was learned about the mind-body connection. Today, we know that the mind and body are interrelated, so much so that empirical research findings can trace physical symptoms of certain illnesses to conscious or unconscious thoughts produced by the mind. Suppressed immune system functioning, high blood pressure, migraine headaches, ulcers, pain, temporary blindness and paralysis, and other physical conditions are all disorders that sometimes have an origin in the processes of the mind."

"OK, I think I follow you, Pearl. But how does that help me golf better?" Buck questioned. "Why does Ty suggest to stop thinking before swinging? After all, golf is supposedly a thinking person's game, so why do balls end up 'Right in the lumberyard,' as Ty says to Danny, if we are thinking rather than being the ball during our swing? Also, if we stop thinking and become the ball, how is that unifying our mind and body?"

"All great questions, Buck. Let me see if I can address them. Here's why and how: A golf swing is a learned skill, and being such, it develops over time. As with any learned skill, at first, we have to concentrate very hard in order to perform it properly, but after practicing, we begin to automatize the skill. We simply place a goal, or end result, in our mind, and our body performs that function more or less automatically. Think about some skills that you had to work hard to learn but now perform automatically. For example, when was the last time you thought about tying your shoes?"

"I guess I don't really think about it. I just know I want my shoes tied and I do it. There's no real thinking happening."

"Right. You don't have to use your mind to think through the steps: Take laces in hand, cross one lace over the other, make one lace into a loop, etcetera, etcetera. Your body performs the action without having to think through the steps. Thinking about it actually makes it harder. And what about riding a bike? At first, that is a hard skill for someone to learn. But once we learn, we never forget, and we never need to think about it. We just do it."

Buck mulled over this information. "I see your point. But I still am not sure I follow how this relates to golf."

Pearl continued his explanation. "Early in the process of learning how to golf, beginners are taught many aspects of the proper swing that require specific mental concentration and thought: grip, stance, posture, takeaway, wrist cock, downswing, hip turn, uncocking the wrists, follow-through, and so forth. Experienced golfers also go through a similar learning process anytime they tinker with their swing, take a lesson from a pro, or read a magazine that gives instructional suggestions. At first, we have to think about each component of the swing independently, and it takes a great deal of mental effort to coordinate all those individual parts of the swing. Our first few swings are unlikely to be fluid in the least."

"I'll say," Buck chimed in.

"With time and practice, our muscles gradually begin to memorize the movement of the golf swing. Very much like we learn to tie our shoes or ride a bike. As the movement becomes engrained in muscle memory, we need less and less conscious thought to fire those muscles correctly. In fact, they actually function better when we eliminate conscious control over them and trust the muscle memory to do its work. The only thing you need to fire those muscles correctly is a goal, or target behavior."

"Like hitting the ball to the green?" Buck asked.

"Yes, like hitting the ball to the green," Pearl replied.

"Okay, I am with you, Pearl. But being the ball doesn't really mean thinking about nothing, does it?"

"By thinking of nothing, I mean that you shouldn't be thinking about the parts of the swing, the wind, your partners, your last swing, your score, your personal problems or any of the other infinite thoughts that could get in the way of telling your muscles where to send the ball. As I mentioned before, the best thing to focus your mind on is the target to which you want to send the ball. After all, if the ball has any human qualities, it is aware of where it sits and where it goes. By being the ball, you are focusing your mind on the ball and where you want your muscles to send it. You are aligning your mind with the task you want the body to perform, achieving the mind-body unity Ty Webb was referring to when he suggested, 'Be the ball.'"

Buck was looking perplexed again. "How do I know the right target, Pearl?"

"For most people, focusing on a target is not a difficult skill once they learn what they are supposed to do. To choose a suitable target, scan the hole and narrow your shot choices down until you know where you want to hit the ball. Choose as specific a target as possible in the area to which you want to hit the ball. A physical feature of the course or range is often a good target. If a specific target does not appeal to you, make the general target as specific as possible. For example, if you are hitting to the green, mentally section the green into four quadrants: left front, right front, left back, and right back. This gives you four targets on the green, and really, if you count the dead center of the green and the pin, the green has six targets. Trees, bunkers, and posts are other examples of targets that often are in the backgrounds of holes. These targets can help you align your body for position and your mind for becoming the ball."

"I get it. If I am being the ball, I should think of a nice spot where I would like to land."

"That's great, Buck," Pearl said, impressed with his student's marriage of the lesson components.

"OK. After I choose a target, how do I begin to focus my mind on it?"

"Once you have chosen the target, it is a good idea to look at it intently. Make a mental picture of the target in your mind's eye. Once you can look away from the target and still see it in your mind, you are well on your way to becoming the ball. All you have to do now is swing the club."

The confused look came across Buck's face again. Pearl smiled, patiently waiting for his question.

"If I am focusing on the target, how do I begin my swing? Don't I have to think to know when to swing?" Buck asked.

"Excellent question, Buck. To swing, you will have to give your body a simple command to start the swing. The command can be almost anything you wish, but it should be simple enough to allow you to maintain your focus on the target. Thinking the words 'Send it' or 'Target' are good examples. A slight head turn or hip movement also works for some people. Whatever you choose, be sure that it allows you to be able to keep your focus on becoming the ball. Make it something personal and make sure it allows you to be comfortable and confident."

Buck was nodding his head in understanding.

Pearl made a mental check of everything he had hoped to convey in this first lesson. All points were covered. "Buck, you've done a great job learning today. Why don't you give me a summary of what you've learned?"

"I can do that," Buck said with a grin. "To become the ball, you must think like the ball. Focus only on the target. Forget everything else. Once you are focused on the target, trust your body to read your mind. Be confident that your muscles will react properly to the message your mind is sending to them. Then think a little swing thought and swing! It's OK to think a little, but not too much."

"That's right. Buck, you've heard the saying, 'I think, therefore, I am,' right?"

"I've heard that."

"In golf, I also have a saying. It goes like this: I think, therefore, I am..... probably thinking too much."

"And being the ball too little," Buck added.

Pearl laughed at Buck's addition to his saying. "Okay, Buck. Now I want you to practice being the ball. Get 50 range balls. Before you hit each ball, choose a target, and practice becoming the ball. Don't hit the ball until you are sure you've become the ball. Also, don't worry about how well or how poorly you hit the shots. That will come with time. Right now, I just want you to practice becoming the ball before each shot."

"Pearl, I'll do better than that. I'll hit a hundred and fifty balls!"

"No," Pearl said firmly. "If you hit that many, there is a good chance you will get tired and hit some balls without doing a quality job of becoming the ball. That is not productive, and it teaches bad habits. I want you to hit fifty only. Make sure you do a good job of focusing on a target and becoming the ball before each shot."

"All right, but I think hitting a hundred and fifty would be better."

Pearl attempted a different tack. "Buck would you be happy two-putting every green?"

"Yes."

"And would you like to shoot a seventy-two?"

"Yes, I would."

"And how many shots is seventy-two minus thirty-six?"

Buck churned the mental machinery. "Thirty-six."

"So if you golfed a round, you would be happy hitting only thirty-six shots, but on the range, you feel you need to hit over one hundred more

17

balls?" Pearl let this idea sink into Buck's skull. "I think you should get used to hitting fifty quality shots and leaving it at that."

As Buck sprinted off to the clubhouse to buy range balls, he heard Pearl shout his final advice for the lesson: "If you feel you need more practice being the ball, I suggest you try it while putting!"

"Pearl's Pearls"

Old Pearl says to remember these tips to become the ball:

1. Pick a specific target for each shot.
2. Always make a good mental picture of your target.
3. Make sure your physical alignment to the target is good.
4. *Be the ball* by focusing only on your target - put all other thoughts aside.
5. Trust your muscles to make a good swing. Be confident. Relax. Let things happen. And be the ball.

Chapter 4: While we're young!

Filmwork

The Scene: Al Czervik's loud, boorish personality doesn't appeal to Judge Smails haughty view of Bushwood. The two men already have clashed once - when Czervik oozed into the Bushwood pro shop and ordered "two a doze, four a doze," and "a box a naked lady tees," and insinuated that one should receive a free bowl of soup if one were to purchase the hideous hat the Judge was wearing - and their second confrontation is imminent. As Czervik impatiently waits for Smails's group to hit, the judge begins a series of ridiculous looking waggles and gyrations and takes his sweet time preparing to drive the ball.

The Quote: Czervik to Smails: "Let's go, while we're young!"

The Lesson: Develop a Preshot Routine

A preshot routine is a series of thoughts, actions, and/or images produced by a golfer prior to hitting the ball. It helps eliminate distractions and prepares the mind and body for the upcoming shot. Ultimately, the preshot routine should be the thing that relates the upcoming shot to all the shots you have taken before. It should remind you that you have done this before, are comfortable and confident doing it, and can do it well.

"Tee one up, Buck," Pearl said.

Buck looked at Pearl suspiciously.

"No tricks this time." Pearl reassured. "Just tee one up and hit it."

Buck did as he was instructed. He set a ball on the tee, took four practice swings, stepped up, shifted his feet, and drove the ball. He struck it well, but it hooked into the rough on the left side of the fairway.

"Not bad," Pearl praised. "Hit another."

Buck realized that he hadn't tried to become the ball on his last swing. By asking him to hit another ball, Pearl must be testing him to see if he learned his first lesson. This time, Buck teed his ball and looked down the fairway, picking a target. Then he took two good practice swings. Next, he stepped up to the ball, took one last look down the fairway, and drove the ball. It faded into a fairway bunker.

"Nice shot. Hit one more."

Buck smiled to himself. He came to learn the mental game, yet Pearl always had a trick up his sleeve to begin the lesson. What did the old man want to see? Buck did his best to figure out what Pearl wanted him to do. He took a long look down the fairway, making sure to hold his gaze long enough so that Pearl would know he was selecting a target. Stepping into a good position a few feet from the ball, he took two good practice swings. Then he stepped forward, setting up over the ball. Again, he looked down the fairway at his target, making sure that Pearl would notice him looking at the target. When he looked back down at the ball, he felt a little uncomfortable, so he shifted his feet a few times and waggled the club, all the while trying to picture his target, becoming the ball. Finally, when he felt he was being the ball, he took his swing and hit a dribbling drive to the right of the fairway.

Buck looked at Pearl and shrugged.

"You'll get there, just keep working on it," Pearl recommended. "Besides, we're not done with you yet. Tell me about each of your shots."

"They were all bad," Buck huffed.

"Tell me more."

"Well, I hit a hook, a fade, and a worm-burner," Buck explained. "None of them were very good shots."

"Mmmhmm," Pearl hummed. "How about before the shot? Tell me about what you did before each shot."

"Oh, I was trying to be the ball."

"Yes, I noticed you picking out your target. That was good."

Buck was pleased.

"But tell me about what you *did* before each shot," Pearl requested.

"What I *did*?" Buck asked.

"Yes, what you did - your physical actions. What did you do before each shot?" Pearl again requested.

"I guess I don't know exactly what I did. I picked a target, took a few practice swings, set up, and swung. That's all I remember."

"Mmmhmm. That's part of the problem," Pearl lectured. "You don't know what you did because you don't get ready to swing in a consistent manner. You don't have a good preshot routine. You're as inconsistent as Judge Smails."

"Preshot routine? What's that?" Buck asked.

Pearl stepped onto his soapbox. "A preshot routine is a series of thoughts, actions, and images produced by a golfer just before he or she takes a shot."

"English, please," Buck requested.

Pearl continued. "A preshot routine is what you do or think before you hit the ball. A good preshot routine helps eliminate distractions, and it prepares the mind and body for the upcoming shot. Ultimately, the preshot routine should be the thing that relates the upcoming shot to all the shots you have taken before. It should remind you that you have done this before and can do it well. As you begin your preshot routine, you should be able to feel your confidence grow, knowing, or at least fooling yourself into believing, that you have made thousands of great shots before."

Buck nodded slowly.

"Tell me, from the filmwork we just did, why do you think I say that the Judge's preshot routine is not a good one?"

Buck tapped a finger to his temple and scrunched his face in thought. "For one thing, I don't think there's any way that he could do the same thing each time. He's all over the place."

"Good."

"Also, he doesn't seem to be comfortable or confident."

21

Pearl nodded thoughtfully. "You're pretty insightful, Buck. That was a good analysis of the Judge's preshot routine. Let's see if you can be equally insightful with your own preshot routine."

"My preshot routine? You told me I don't have a routine yet, Pearl."

"Mmm, that's true. You don't really have one yet, but that's fine, Buck. We can develop one for you very easily. Let's do some planning." Pearl suggested.

"Okay."

"The purpose of a preshot routine is to prepare your mind and body for the upcoming shot. A good preshot routine will help you focus your mind on the target, set your attitude for the shot, and eliminate as many distractions as possible. It should relax you and remind you to trust your swing, allowing you to feel confident that your upcoming shot is the same as any of the other hundreds or thousands of great shots you have played."

"That seems like a lot to do in only a few seconds," Buck said.

"I guess it does," Pearl realized. "But remember this Buck: As you go through the same routine time after time, you will get better at it. Also, there is no single perfect preshot routine, what works for one golfer doesn't necessarily work for anyone else. For you, we can make the preshot routine very simple. But first, we need to do a little work before we can simplify things. Buck, I want you to hit about ten balls, paying attention to what you see, hear, feel, and think. That part is very important. Don't worry too much about having a preshot routine yet. Just pick a target and hit them as you normally would."

Buck did as he was told. For each shot, he tried to pick a target and take a few good practice swings before hitting the ball. He was careful to note the sensations he was seeing, hearing, feeling, and thinking.

"Okay Buck, that was good. Tell me, what did you see?" Pearl asked.

"Well, I tried to pick a target, and keep that target in my mind. I used it to help become the ball."

"Very good. Anything else?"

Buck shook his head.

"OK, what did you hear before or during your shots?"

"Nothing much. Some noise on the course and the noise I made with my swings, but nothing that distracted me."

"That's good. How about what you felt? What were your feelings?"

"Well, I felt a little nervous, like I always do when someone is watching me. It makes my hands grip the club tightly, I think."

"Mmmhmm, some tension," Pearl observed. "Go on."

"Like you said, I was just a little tense. I felt like my swing was a little choppy because my muscles were tight."

"How about what you were thinking?" Pearl asked.

"I was thinking a lot about how I felt a little tense and how my swing is not very good. I also was trying to think about all the other things you told me to notice, so I was probably thinking too much to do a good job of becoming the ball."

"Great observations, Buck," Pearl praised. "You really did a great job with that exercise. Let's see if we can get a good preshot routine out of that information." Pearl set a ball in front of Buck and stepped back. "Buck, when we began, what did you tell me about the way you wanted to hit the ball?"

"I wanted to grip it and rip it like Rich Daddy!"

"That's right. I think we need to design a preshot routine that will get you confident in your ability to step up to the ball and grip it and rip it," Pearl said.

"We can do that?" Buck asked.

"Sure," said Pearl. "A preshot routine should fit the person using it. If you get a good feeling out of gripping it and ripping it, then we should go with that. We just need to make sure that we can do a few other things too."

"Like what?" Buck asked.

"Like picking a target, focusing, and trusting your grip it and rip it swing."

"Okay, how do we do that?"

"What is the first thing you think you should do?"

23

"Pick my target," Buck answered thoughtfully.

"Very good," Pearl said. He was pleased with Buck's answer. "So the first thing we need to do is pick a target. Do that now."

Buck dropped a ball, stepped behind it, and looked down the fairway. He picked a spot in the fairway with a distant tree directly behind it. "Okay, got one. Now what."

"Did you like the way you picked the target, from behind the ball?" Pearl asked.

"I guess."

"Some people pick their target from right next to the ball. It doesn't matter which perspective you choose as long as it makes you comfortable. Now, step up to the ball at a practice swing distance, making sure your feet and shoulders are aligned properly."

Buck did as instructed.

"Now Buck, we have come to an important part of the preshot routine. You need to make some practice swings that will allow you to trust your swing and focus on the upcoming shot. If possible, remind yourself of similar shots you have made before, and be confident that you can do it again. If you need to talk to yourself in your mind at this point, go ahead and do that. Is there a saying you might want to tell yourself?"

"Grip it and rip it, I guess." Buck indicated.

"Good. Make a few swings saying that to yourself. And Buck, be confident. You are getting better by the second, and you will be a very good golfer before you know it."

Buck made a few swings while telling himself to grip it and rip it. He thought about a great drive he hit on this hole last year.

"OK, step up to the ball making sure your feet and shoulders are lined up properly," Pearl instructed. "How do you feel?"

"A little tense," Buck admitted.

"Let's try this: Lift the clubhead off the ground and waggle it a few times. Make sure your grip is relaxed, and repeat to yourself, 'Grip it.'"

Buck did as Pearl suggested.

"Now, you should try to become the ball, focus on your target. Take one last look down the fairway at your target, and burn that target into your mind. Make sure you have a good picture of it in your head. You can even do this while you waggle the club if it is comfortable to you."

Buck took a look down the fairway and spotted his target. He waggled the club a few times, reminding himself to grip it lightly yet securely.

"Now tell yourself to, 'Rip it,' and start your swing. The swing should come automatically because you trust it so much you don't even have to think about it once you start your backswing. You are thinking only about your target."

Buck stepped back. "Pearl, that is a lot to think about right before swinging. How can I be the ball and do all the other stuff at the same time?"

Pearl smiled. "It will be easier when I'm not talking so much. Also, you'll get better and more relaxed the more times you do it. Start from the top and see if you can do it."

Buck stepped back and picked out his target. Next, he stepped into practice swing position, making sure he was lined up correctly. He took a few swings, reminding himself to grip it and rip it. In his mind, he saw himself making a great shot - like one he made last summer - that landed right on target. Next, he stepped up to the ball. He waggled the club and looked at his target, all the while repeating to himself to grip it, feeling a relaxed grip on the club. When he felt his arms and hands relax, he grounded the clubhead. Seeing the target in his mind, Buck told himself, 'Rip it,' and he started his swing. His drive landed left of his target, but it was in the fairway.

"Great job, Buck," Pearl praised. "That was a very good preshot routine. The shot was pretty good too. How did it feel?"

"It felt pretty good. I like telling myself to grip it and rip it. It's like having my own personal preshot routine."

"It is having your own personal preshot routine. That's the point," Pearl corrected. "We'll keep working on it, too. You'll get even better after a few more lessons."

Buck laughed. He knew he was getting better even though he hadn't hit any range balls today. He felt great knowing that he was working hard to improve his game. "That routine really is pretty simple, but I think it helps. I sure don't look like Judge Smails. And I'll never have to hear somebody yell, 'While we're young!'"

"Pearl's Pearls"

Pearl says to grab a club and go through these steps to develop a solid preshot routine:

1. Remember this and you know all you need to know: A good preshot routine will incorporate the fundamental grip, stance, and alignment to prepare you physically for the shot, and it will allow you to become confident, relaxed, and focused.

2. Take some time to figure out a few thoughts or actions that make you feel relaxed. Put one in your preshot routine.

3. Think of a few thoughts or actions that make you feel confident in your swing. Put one in your preshot routine.

4. Figure out how you want to choose your target and become the ball. Incorporate that action into your preshot routine.

5. The preshot routine is a great action to align not only your mind, but also your body for the upcoming shot. Make sure a good fundamental grip, stance, and alignment is part of your preshot routine. Note: It is not necessary to make a practice swing a part of your preshot routine, but it might help, especially for putts and less than full shots.

6. Practice hitting some balls using a few of your ideas for choosing a target, becoming the ball, using good fundamentals, and feeling relaxed and confident. Put your favorite thoughts and actions together into a simple, personalized preshot routine.

7. After you develop a preshot routine with which you are comfortable, use it before hitting each shot (on the range or the course). If you find that an element of the routine doesn't work for you, change it. But remember, just like developing your swing, developing your preshot routine takes time and practice. Inconsistency in your preshot routine will breed inconsistency in your shot making. Consistency in your preshot routine will produce consistency in your shot making.

Chapter 5: Nananananaaaaaa

Filmwork

The Scene: Ty is putting on the green, amazing Danny with his astounding shot making ability. Ty holes ball after ball, regardless of his choice of putting implement. "Nananananaaaaaa," Ty putts several in. "Nananananananaaaaa," Ty kicks one in with his foot. "Nananananaaaaa," he shoots one in using his putter like a pool cue. Ty is on an amazing roll before he finally misses one. Then, just as easily as he holed the previous balls, he putts in one last ball, jumping it over another en route to the cup.

The Quote: Ty Webb: "Nananananananaaaaaaaaaaaa."

The Lesson: Confidence is King

In order to become a great golfer, you must be confident. It is the key to improving and maintaining your game. And despite what you might think, you can become confident before you become good.

Out on the practice green, Pearl putted a few balls before beginning his lesson. Buck watched him carefully. On each attempt, Pearl eyed the line of the putt carefully, took four practice swings, stepped into place, eyed the putt again, then gently swung the putter like a pendulum, sending the ball rolling slowly toward the hole. After three eight-footers in a row, he looked up at Buck. "Pretty nice putting performance Ty put on, hey Buck?"

"Pretty nice is right," Buck agreed.

"Buck, who do you think is the best putter in the game today?"

"I wouldn't bet against Tiger," Buck indicted. "He's a pretty good putter."

"He's pretty good at chipping too," Pearl added.

Buck nodded in agreement.

"Buck, what do Tiger and Ty Webb have in common?" Pearl questioned.

"Their both tall?" Buck's inflection made the answer into a question.

"True, but not what I was looking for." Pearl attacked the lesson from a different angle. "Buck, why do you think Tiger and Ty are so much better than you at the short game?" Pearl asked.

"That's easy," Buck said. "They have better strokes, much better."

"Mmm, that they do. But I don't think that's the main reason they have a much better short game than you do." Pearl mused.

"Do you think it's because they read the greens better?" Buck asked.

"Certainly, Tiger and Ty read the greens much better than you do," Pearl agreed. "And they have caddies to help them read the greens." Pearl scrunched up his face and scratched his head for effect. He paused slightly between words. "But still, if you had the best caddy in the world and a stroke equal to Tiger's, either one of them would still be much better around the greens."

"They would?" Buck said, confused as ever. "How could they be if we were equal?"

"I gave you an equal stroke and a perfect caddy to read the greens, but I didn't give you everything they have. What would you be missing?" Pearl challenged.

Buck thought out loud. "If I had Tiger's stroke and the perfect caddy, I guess the only other things I would need are Tiger's clubs. So I'll say his clubs."

"Confident in your answer?" Pearl asked with a furrowed brow.

"No," Buck admitted quietly as he hung his head in defeat.

"Nor are you in your game. That's why you'd be beaten by Tiger," Pearl said sternly. "Or Ty for that matter," he added for emphasis.

Buck stood stupefied. "I don't get it. If we were equal in every area but confidence, how would they still beat me? What is the big deal about confidence?"

With the key question in place, Pearl began his sermon. "I think confidence is the single most important attribute of a good mental golf game. Confidence underlies many of the other important aspects of the game and ties them together. Let me explain." Pearl held out his right index finger and crossed it with his left, as if counting off number one. "First, let's look at what confidence does for the swing. In order to swing properly, we need to be willing to release conscious control of our swing. Once the swing has been committed to muscle memory, we only need to trigger those muscles to do their job and let them go to work. If we try to consciously think about the movements of our swing, we become too tentative, and a choppy, over-controlled swing is the result. Confidence in our swing allows us to trust our muscle memory and release conscious control of our swing, allowing the muscles to work effectively to produce a smooth, repeatable swing." Pearl counted off number two with his fingers. "Second, when we are confident, we free our conscious mind to focus on the target, sending signals to our muscles telling them to *send the ball there*," he accentuated the last phrase.

Pearl studied Buck's face to see whether he was getting the message. The dog-like tilt of Buck's head told him that further explanation was needed. "Come on, Buck," he said. "Let's hit the range for some examples of confidence in action."

Being a Saturday morning, Pearl knew that Rich Daddy would be swinging away on the range, confident as ever. He took Buck over to the range and set up class a few yards behind Rich Daddy, who smiled when he saw them.

"Hello, fellows," Rich Daddy bellowed. "Come for a lesson today?" he asked Buck.

"Yes I did," Buck replied cheerfully.

"Rich," Pearl started, "Would you mind telling Young Buck here just how you became such a good golfer?"

Rich Daddy furrowed his brow in thought. "Well," he began, "I guess it was a long process."

"Tell us about it," Pearl encouraged.

"It started with some lessons from Club Pro. Those lessons helped a lot. But then when I took some lessons from you, Pearl, I got much better over the next few years."

"Tell us about your lessons from me. How did it help to have them?"

"At first, I was a little confused by the lessons, but then it took off. You told me I could be good, and I believed it. Then I looked at some other good golfers at the club. They didn't seem any different from me in any important way, and I said to myself, 'Why not me?' After that, I started playing better, and I just kept getting better. With every good shot, my confidence grew. Pretty soon, I was Club Champion."

"That's impressive," Pearl marveled. "Tell us, when you play in the Club Championship, how do you feel?"

"I feel confident!" Rich Daddy said with authority, causing Buck's jaw to drop. "I feel confident, and I just grip it and rip it. That's the secret."

Now Rich Daddy was talking Buck's language, and his interest was piqued. "You mean, gripping it and ripping it is all about confidence?" Buck asked.

"I should say so. How else would you be able to grip it and rip it if you weren't confident?"

Buck had never thought of it that way. He always thought that Rich Daddy seemed confident *because he grips and rips*. Now, Rich Daddy was saying the opposite: He grips and rips *because he is confident*. The confidence came first for Rich Daddy! Buck had finally realized why he had never been able to grip it and rip it well: He lacked the confidence to do it well. Now he only had one problem standing in the way of him becoming a golfer like Rich Daddy.

"Rich Daddy, can I ask you something?" Buck said sincerely.

"Sure, Buck. Go ahead."

"How did you become confident before you became a good golfer?"

Rich Daddy threw back his head and laughed a deep, hearty laugh. He knew something Buck didn't. "That's what this guy is for," he said, pointing to Pearl. "He's the master."

Buck looked at Pearl, who stood smiling to himself, smugly confident in his own ability as a teacher of golf's mental game. By the glint in Buck's eye, Pearl could see he had an eager pupil. That was good.

"Do you think you can become a good golfer, Buck?" Pearl asked.

"I do, Pearl. In time, I really think I can become a very good golfer." Buck urged.

Pearl smiled knowingly. "You're already on you're way there, Buck. You have great expectancy."

"Great what?" Buck asked.

"Expectancy," said Pearl. "Let me explain." Pearl explained to Buck that expectancy is a major principle in medicine and psychotherapy, and it can help one gain confidence in their golf game before he or she actually becomes a good ball striker. Any good therapist or healer knows that he or she is more likely to help a client improve their state of being if they can plant a seed that makes the client believe he or she will get better. It is the client's expectation that they will get better that actually aids in the healing process. Pearl illustrated expectancy by relating it to a concept called the *placebo effect*, a concept with which Buck a minimal familiarity. Pearl said that when medical researchers test drugs, they usually do a double-blind study in which they assign research participants with a particular problem to one of two groups: one group gets the real drug being tested and the other group gets a sugar pill known as a placebo. Neither the researchers nor the research participants know who is being given the real drug and who is being given the placebo, hence the term double-blind. Conventional wisdom says that if the drug works, 100 percent of the people getting the drug will get better and none of the people getting the placebo will get better. However, what actually happens is this: Less than 100 hundred percent of the people getting the real drug get better and about 35 percent of the people getting the placebo get better. It is theorized that the 35 percent of the placebo group get better because they believe they are getting the real deal, which they assume will make them better. It is commonly believed that it is their expectancy that they will get better that actually makes their symptoms improve. In other words, they get better simply because they believe that they will get better. This expectancy effect is seen in medical research of physical symptoms and also psychological research of mental symptoms. It is a real and consistent effect found in the research.

Pearl finished his placebo effect dissertation by encouraging Buck to keep up his great attitude. "Buck, you can take advantage of the placebo effect by allowing yourself to be confident in your abilities and efforts. Before, when you were doing nothing to improve, I didn't blame you for not being confident. You were just setting proper expectations for yourself. But if you are willing to work to improve, and you must be because you asked me for help, then you must believe that what you are doing is going to help you improve. Not only will your belief open the door for new possibilities, the simple act of believing has the power to make you improve, regardless of anything else you do! That's the power of expectancy. So be confident that your efforts are going to make you a better player. They will!"

"That's great!" Buck said excitedly. "I do expect to improve, but..." he paused, "I don't really have any confidence in my game right now. How will I become confident in my swing?"

Pearl had an answer for everything. "I've explained to you how confidence allows us to free our muscles from conscious control and swing fluidly, but to me the most compelling reason for extolling the virtues of confidence comes from the concept of self efficacy."

Buck was growing a little tired of Pearl's fifty-cent words, but he was learning. He decided to indulge the old man. "Self-what-acy?"

"Self efficacy. In simple terms, self efficacy is the belief one has in his or her abilities to achieve a certain outcome. Basically, your self-efficacy is the level of confidence you feel about achieving a certain goal. The greater our self-efficacy the greater likelihood we have of achieving our goals. For now, we'll just call it confidence."

"Great. Now I just need to get some."

"Oh we'll get you some," Pearl said confidently. "There are four basic ways to improve confidence. The first way to improve confidence is performance accomplishment, or the act of achieving a goal. It stands to reason that if we want to achieve something, we will be more confident in our ability to achieve it if we have achieved it before. The more we do something, the more we believe that we are capable of doing it again. Notice that this can work against us too. The more we slice, the more we start to believe that we will slice again. That is why I recommend to always focus on the correct way to do things and forget about what you are doing wrong. Remember, there are millions of ways to screw something up, but you only need to find one way to do it right."

Buck nodded, a good sign. Pearl continued.

"The second way to improve confidence is to learn vicariously by watching someone else do it. There are a couple of ways to improve your confidence vicariously. One way is by watching good playing partners and seeing what they do correctly."

Rich Daddy had gone back to striking range balls, but upon hearing Pearl's last statement, he decided to add his own two cents. "I learned by watching Pearl," he said, causing a sudden inflation in Pearl's ego. Rich Daddy watched the palpable inflation with eager anticipation. "I figured, if an old fuddy duddy like him can be a good golfer, why not me?" The deflation of Pearl's ego was rapid enough to cause a slight breeze on the range. "Find other people you identify with who are good at golf. Picture yourself doing the things they are doing. When they do something well, you need to tell yourself, 'If they can do it, why can't I? I'll do it too!'"

Pearl, still reeling a little from Rich Daddy's jab, continued his lesson. "Watching the pros play golf is another way to increase confidence. When you watch them make great shots, picture yourself making those same shots. Allow yourself some vicarious accomplishment by pretending that you can make those shots too. Even if it is difficult at first, keep trying to imagine yourself making great shots like the pros. Push out the negative images and replace them with visions of success."

"What if I can't even imagine success?" Buck asked.

"You will, even if it takes some practice. For those who can't even imagine that they are capable of great shots, I can give an immediate diagnosis of their problem as a golfer: They lack the smallest level of

34

confidence possible and may as well give up golf before they become extremely miserable. They should find another hobby, one in which they can imagine success."

Pearl continued. "The third way to improve confidence is through verbal persuasion. Whether you do this yourself or have others help you, persuasion is a powerful tool. We begin to believe the words we speak and the words that are spoken to us. The power of words has been documented in many books, Buck."

"So how do I use that to my advantage?" Buck asked.

"Pay attention to the words you use to describe your game. Are you critical of yourself or encouraging? Do the words you use to describe your game inspire confidence or uncertainty? Also pay attention to your explanations for good and bad shots. You should attribute good shots to things that are personal, pervasive, and permanent. For example, if you hit a good shot, say to yourself, 'I hit that good shot because I am a good golfer. I have a good swing. And I am confident.' When you hit bad shots, learn from it and move on. Forget that bad shots quickly."

Buck thought aloud. "So if I hit a good shot, I should take credit for it and remember it, but if I hit a bad one, I should forget it?"

"Think of it this way, if you make a good shot, remember it and use that memory to increase your confidence that you are a good golfer," Pearl explained. "But if you hit a bad shot, forget it, or explain it as something that isn't permanent and can be fixed."

"That I can do," Buck said with confidence.

"The fourth way to increase confidence is through physical states that produce feelings of efficacy."

"Whoa, you lost me," Buck complained.

"Just think of it as a something you do to make you feel more confident. Taking some deep breaths can have a calming effect, which is usually better for confidence than being anxious."

Rich Daddy couldn't resist chiming in. "I use an anchor to help me feel confident, Buck," he piped loudly.

Buck was curious. "What's an anchor?"

"An anchor is a movement, sight, or sound you use to help you feel more confident. For me, I squeeze my grips and say to myself, 'Grip it and rip it,' before I drive the ball. That helps me get a feeling of confidence because I anchored it a long time ago."

"How did you do that?"

"I recalled great shots that I had made before. Those memories made me feel confident. Then, while I was feeling confident from reliving my glory shots, I squeezed the grips of a club and said to myself, 'Grip it and rip it.' I practiced this several times a day for a week or so. Now, anytime I squeeze my grips or think, 'Grip it and rip it,' I feel more confident."

"Wow," Buck said, marveling at Rich Daddy's ingenuity.

Pearl felt the need to add his two cents. "It's a case of classical conditioning, Buck. You pair a conditioned stimulus with true stimulus to elicit a response. You see, the thoughts of his glorious shots produced a confident response in Rich Daddy. Once he introduced squeezing the grips into this equation, he learned an association between squeezing the grips and feeling confident. Now, anytime he squeezes the grips he begins to feel confident. He did the same thing with the saying, 'Grip it and rip it.'"

"Yeah, stimulus, shmimulus," Rich Daddy said upon noticing Buck's bewildered eyes. "Buck, just know this. Remember some good shots that make you feel confident. Then focus on feeling that confidence as strongly as you can. Then do something or say something that you can easily repeat on the course while keeping that confident feeling. Practice this a few times a day, and soon you'll be able to become confident just by doing or saying something."

"Rich Daddy, you really know your mental game," Buck said with stars in his eyes.

Rich Daddy beamed while Pearl took offense to this exchange, knowing that he taught Rich Daddy everything he knew. Pearl cleared his throat to get Buck's attention - twice. "Okay Buck," Pearl said. "That about covers it. Any questions?"

"Nope. I'm just going to stay here a while and watch Rich Daddy. Just being around him makes me feel confident."

As Pearl walked away he glanced back at Buck, who was mirroring Rich Daddy's every move. Rich shared some range balls with the boy, and the two began work developing an anchor for Buck. Soon, they were gripping away, taking swings, and chanting, "Grip it and rip it!" in unison.

Pearl had to laugh to himself. His two pupils were practicing together, both as confident as could be. With no one else there to congratulate him for his small victory, Pearl reached to the sky, bent his forearm behind his head, and patted himself on the back.

Pearl says to remember these tips to build confidence:

1. Confidence is one of the most important factors in becoming a good golfer. Remember, becoming more confident can be a conscious choice. Any time you feel worry or anxiety about your game, work on replacing that feeling with confidence. Even if you are a poor player now, be confident in your ability to improve. Be confident that your practice habits are making you better. Even by picking up this book and reading it, you are gaining the potential to improve your game. Be confident that you are getting better.

2. Remember the placebo effect. Your expectation that you will improve through your mental or physical play and practice habits is a powerful source of change. Believe that you are improving each and every day. The simple act of believing has the power to make you improve, regardless of anything else you do! That's the power of expectancy. So be confident that your efforts are going to make you a better player. They will!

3. You can improve your confidence, or self-efficacy in other ways as well. Four documented ways include 1) performance accomplishment, 2) vicarious learning, 3) verbal persuasion, and 4) confident physical feelings. By taking advantage of all four of these sources, you can improve your game immensely.

4. Anchoring the feeling of confidence to a physical action, sight, or sound is an easy way to gain confidence. To anchor the feeling of confidence, recall some of your good shots that make you feel confident. Next, focus on feeling that confidence as strongly as you can. Let the feeling of confidence build. To anchor the feeling, do something or say something that you can easily repeat on the course while continuing to feel the confidence within you. Practice this a few times a day, and soon you'll be able to become confident just by triggering your anchor.

Chapter 6: Why Don't You Improve Your Lie?

Filmwork

The Scene: Danny Noonan is caddying for Judge Smails. They are walking near the woods, where the judge's sliced ball has landed. As they walk, the judge attempts to surreptitiously improve the position of his ball by kicking it toward the fairway. Danny notices this and tries to let him off the hook for cheating. The judge takes the hint. He kicks his ball even farther than before and cites "winter rules" as a justification for the improvement of his lie.

The Quote: Noonan: "Why don't you improve your lie a little, sir?"
Smails: "Yes, yes, winter rules."

The Lesson: Imagine Yourself Being Capable of Great Things, Even If You Haven't Accomplished Them Yet

Much like we can use winter rules to improve the lie of our golf ball, an active imagination can help us create a better mental golfing reality for ourselves before we are physically capable of it. A vivid visualization, or lie, about the game we desire can help move us in the direction of making our golfing dreams a reality. Visualize it. Believe it. Then make it come true.

"Have you ever lied about your golf game, Buck?" Pearl asked.

Buck reflected on his less than perfect past etiquette. He searched his mind for an answer that would be palatable to Pearl. "There have been a few times when I might not have counted all my strokes. I remember a few times I topped the ball a few feet and I didn't count it," he admitted.

"Mmmhmm," Pearl nodded. "Any other times?"

"Maybe a few," Buck said quietly. He was embarrassed to admit that he regularly shaved a stroke or two off several holes a round.

Pearl looked out at the horizon. He sat quietly for a moment, letting Buck's anxious tension eat away at him. "You know, Buck, there was a time when I used to shave a few strokes off my game every round."

Buck's eyes grew large. "You did?" he said incredulously.

"Yes I did," Pearl admitted. "A few times a game, when I hit very poor shots or hit into a hazard, I might not count a stroke here or there. Not every time, but enough that it made me a worse player."

Buck frowned. "How did not counting strokes make you a worse player? Didn't it make your score lower?"

"Yes it did. But in the end, because I was lying to myself about how good my scores were getting, I didn't focus on the parts of my game that were weak. I was living a lie, not being honest about the sad state of my golf game. Ultimately, I became a worse player."

Buck thought for a moment. "But Pearl, you're a great player now. How did you improve your game so much?" Buck asked, eager to learn Pearl's secret.

"I starting telling better lies," Pearl said matter of factly.

Buck raised his eyebrows and leaned forward toward the old man. He tried to imagine Pearl improving his cheating techniques. "Pearl, what in the world do you mean? There must be a trick."

"There is." Pearl got up and went to his bag. He took out a ball, dropped it on the tee box, and proceeded to slice it into a patch of trees lining the fairway. Then without a word he smiled at Buck, turned on his heel, and strolled after it.

Buck looked on with a confused, irritated look on his face as Pearl leisurely pursued his ball. When Pearl got about fifty yards away, Buck called to him. The old man didn't answer. Buck shook his head started to follow. "Wait up," he called.

When teacher and student finally found the ball, it was resting in a thick bed of grass behind a large oak. Under the mighty oak, Pearl began the sermon. "In our filmwork today, we saw the judge attempt to improve the position of his ball by kicking it toward the fairway." Pearl kicked the ball toward the fairway and sauntered after it. As he was walking toward the ball he casually looked from side to side as if he were looking for someone watching him. As he walked near the ball, he kicked it in stride toward the fairway. "Danny notices the judge kicking the ball and tries to let him off the hook for cheating. Danny says....." Pearl waited for Buck to chime in with the line of the lesson.

"Why don't you improve your lie a little, sir?" Buck said on cue.

"Mmmhmm," Pearl nodded. "The judge takes the hint. He kicks his ball even farther than before and cites 'winter rules' as a justification for the improvement of his lie." Pearl kicked the ball once more in stride. "Yes, yes, winter rules," Pearl huffed in his best Judge Smails voice as he kicked the ball.

Buck watched in bewilderment as Pearl walked toward the ball, now near the fairway. "Are you telling me to cheat?" he asked.

"No, not at all," Pearl said innocently. "I'm trying to give you the same advice Danny gave the judge. I'm telling you to improve your lie."

Buck's furrowed brow indicated that an explanation was necessary.

"How many lies are going on here?" Pearl nudged.

Buck scratched his head. Being fed up with the old man's antics, he gave up quickly. "I don't know."

"Let me ask this then," Pearl said, not letting Buck off the hook easily, "How many different types of lies do we have in our little lesson so far?"

Buck thought back to the beginning of the lesson when Pearl had mentioned lying about his scores. Then he looked at Pearl standing over his ball, which was sitting pretty on a verdant patch of freshly mowed fairway. "Two," he replied.

"Now you're starting to get it," Pearl said. "Let me explain further. In this scene, we see that the judge, the apparent arbiter of justice, believes that special rules come into play where he is concerned. He shows no shame in cheating to give himself an unfair advantage over his opponents. In essence, the judge is telling a *lie,* to his opponents, concealing the truth behind his cheating, to improve the *lie* of his ball. Although the judge's tactics may be less than ethical, we are going to look at the underlying principles of his actions to find a sterling example of sport psychology in action. We'll see how you can use the judge's example to improve some lies of your own. Without even bending a rule, I'll show you how improving your *lie*, a false statement, will improve your *lie*, the resting position of the ball."

"How can lying improve my game?" Buck asked.

"Henry Ford once said, 'Whether you think you can or think you can't, you're right.' And there's something to that. The use of imagery, or visualization, can be used to create a mental picture of something you want to accomplish. The images you generate can actually send signals to your muscles, telling them what you want them to perform. This is a powerful tool for enhancing your swing mechanics and overall ability to hit the ball to a specific target."

"Where's the lie come in? When do I lie to myself?" Buck questioned.

Pearl expounded on his theory. "If you think about it, imagery really is just a vivid lie we tell ourselves. For the most part, we imagine shots we have not taken yet, and we do our best to believe that we will make that shot come true. We sit in our living room or stand on the tee box imagining a perfect shot that probably won't happen. Still, if we are good at it, we start to make shots very close to what we are imaging. Think and you will become. In other words, if we start to believe the lie we tell ourselves through the imagery we create, we will change our actions to make that lie come true. It's a self-fulfilling prophecy."

"Are you saying that if I can imagine myself hitting a shot, I will hit that shot?" Buck asked.

"You won't always hit the shot you imagine, but using imagery will improve your chances of hitting the shot you desire," Pearl explained.

"So by visualizing myself making great shots, I can fool myself into believing I am a better golfer than I am," Buck reasoned. "And if I believe I am a good golfer, I will become a good golfer."

"Something like that," Pearl reassured. "The key is to make the most vivid images possible, so you truly start to believe them. When you visualize yourself becoming a great golfer, make sure you really *feel* it.

Vividly imagine the shots you will make, the sounds you will hear, the feelings you will have. The better the lie you tell yourself, the better your lies will be."

Buck stood still, staring off into the horizon, absorbing this information. Pearl let him reflect for a minute or so before he began again.

"Let's take imagery a step further and combine it with another important concept: confidence. If we can use imagery to enhance our actions, why not use it to enhance our feelings? Imagery can be used to create impulses in our muscles. In essence, our thoughts can actually fire those muscle fibers, tricking them into thinking they are doing something they are not really doing at all. It is all in your mind, but the body does not know that. Believing that we are capable of great accomplishments will increase our confidence in our abilities."

"So lying to myself will increase my confidence?"

Pearl paused and searched for a way to elaborate his concept. "In a way it will. In our previous lesson on confidence, you learned about self-efficacy and ways to improve it. Pop quiz: What was the number one way to improve self efficacy?"

Buck searched his memory for the answer. "Doing something?"

"That's right. It was performance accomplishment. The best way to increase self-efficacy is to perform something correctly."

Buck nodded.

"Based on what we know about self-efficacy, there is bad news and good news. The bad news is that doing something correctly is sometimes easier *said* than done. The good news is that doing something correctly is also easier *seen* than done."

Pearl continued. "Great athletes use imagery to increase their confidence all the time. They picture the results of their performance before they happen, and then they go out and try to accomplish what they have imagined. When they find themselves in the position to do something great, they are not unnerved because they have been in that situation before, even if only in their imagination. The outcome is familiar to them, and they have confidence that it will occur because they have pictured it so vividly in their imagination.

"Many people who have accomplished great things have said that they did so because they had a strong belief that they would be successful. These people have powerful visions of the future and they work hard to make their visions come true. They succeed because they persevere and have confidence. In other words, they imagined a possibility, a lie if you will, and made it come true."

"How come visualization is so powerful, Pearl?"

"From a neurological standpoint, the brain has difficulty distinguishing what is real from what is imagined. The information that is imagined is treated in much the same way that visual, auditory, and motor-input is handled - it's all sensory information. In other words, something real and something imagined are treated in basically the same way by our central nervous system. We can take advantage of this situation by imagining the greatest scenarios possible. If we repeatedly imagine great outcomes, we can strengthen our belief that we have the power to make those outcomes come true."

"So if I visualize well, my brain actually might think I have done something I haven't? And that will make me a more confident and better golfer?"

"Yes, it can. But don't think of visualization as seeing something you haven't actually done, think of it as a vision of what you will do in the future."

"Pearl, this seems to good to be true. I mean, you're telling me that all I have to do is see something in my mind and I can make it come true."

Pearl laughed. "Buck, if you put it that way, it is too good to be true. Put it this way, if you use visualization, it will help you accomplish what you imagine. But you need to add some things to that visualization for it to come true." Pearl paused.

Buck couldn't contain his enthusiasm. "What? What do you need to add?" he demanded.

"Hard work and persistence." Pearl took a club from his bag and addressed the ball. He gazed at the green for a few seconds then took a practice swing before settling over the ball. With a fluid, graceful swing, Pearl struck down on the ball, sending it in a beautiful arc toward the green. The ball bounced once then checked up quickly, settling ten feet from the pin. Pearl smiled and walked toward the green, leaving Buck to gape at the amazing shot.

When Pearl reached the green, Buck had caught up with him. They huddled near the ball.

"Now Buck, I could see myself making shots like that long before I could actually make them. It took practice and patience to become a very good player. Do you understand what I'm saying?"

Buck nodded.

"If you can see it in your mind, you can make it happen through hard work and persistence. But if you can't see it in your mind, you will never make it happen. You might get lucky from time to time, but you'll never become an excellent golfer."

"Okay, so how do I learn to see it? How does one get good at visualizing?" Buck asked.

"Visualization really is very simple" Pearl said. "All you have to do is create a vivid image in your mind. Imagine the swing and game that you want to have. Make it come true in your mind. Make up the greatest lie you can."

"Is there something specific I should think about?"

"Not really, but you have to make the image as vivid as possible. Imagine the sights, sounds, smells, feels, and feelings of the game you want to have. When you can do that and feel comfortable with it and believe it, you are doing a good job. Then when you get out on the course, use visualization to help you imagine your shot and become the ball. It will get easier with practice."

Pearl knelt behind his putt and eyed his line to the cup. Then he stepped up to the ball. He made the putt for a 3, plus the use of the foot wedge. Buck shook his head in amazement.

"I do suggest one other guideline for using visualization, Buck."

"What's that?"

"You have to relax. Imagery works best when you are relaxed. So get comfortable before you do it. Take a few breaths from the diaphragm to help your body relax."

"I'm not sure I have one of those, Pearl," Buck said with a deadpan expression.

Pearl laughed. "Your diaphragm is a sheet of muscle that runs beneath your lungs. Using it to help you breathe increases the amount of oxygen you bring into your lungs, which helps you relax. Breathe slowly and deeply while placing one hand on your chest and one on your stomach. You should breath so that only the hand on your stomach moves up and down. Like this." Pearl demonstrated with a few breaths then helped Buck do it himself. "After you learn how to do this, you won't need the hands to help you."

"And I should do that every time I use visualization?" Buck asked with hesitation in his voice. "Pearl, I think my buddies will have a field day with that one."

Pearl shook his head. "Use the breathing at home. It will greatly help you relax and put your mind and body into an agreeable state to believe your imagined lie. On the course, you won't want to use the hands, but by then, you'll have learned how to take a few good deep breaths."

As they walked off the green toward the next hole, Buck asked, "Pearl, how do I know if I tell a lie that's too good for me to achieve?"

Pearl thought for moment before he gave his answer. "I wouldn't worry about that, Buck. Most people have no trouble ratcheting their expectations down. But many have trouble truly believing that they are capable of accomplishing the high expectations they set for themselves. That's why they don't accomplish them. They don't truly believe their goals are within their reach."

Both thought about Pearl's words as they continued their walk to the next hole.

Pearl continued. "If you ever get stuck, just remember the name of this lesson: improve your lie. If your lie isn't working, change it. Improve it. Maybe you need to make it more believable, maybe you need to make the sights, sounds, feels, smells, and feelings more clearly visible. But whatever you do, make sure you are always working to improve your game, believing you are capable of a better game."

Buck nodded in agreement. "To improve your lie, improve your lie."

Old Pearl says to remember these tips to improve your lie:

1. Be honest with yourself about your strengths and weaknesses, but overestimate your potential. Make it a great lie you tell yourself, then set out to make it come true.

2. Imagine that you are capable of great things by visualizing yourself doing them. Allow your confidence in your abilities to grow by visualizing yourself accomplishing the game you desire. If you imagine a scenario vividly, your mind cannot tell the difference between things you have actually done and those you only have imagined. Remember what Henry Ford said: "Whether you think you can or think you can't, you are right."

3. To make the most of visualization, relax. Lie or sit still and breathe deeply from the diaphragm to begin physiological relaxation (To feel the correct execution of this movement, put one hand on your stomach and one on your chest. Practice breathing so that only the hand on your stomach moves up and down with your breath). Allow yourself to relax, which puts your mind and body into an agreeable state to believe your imagined lie.

4. Visualize vividly. Imagine the sights, sounds, smells, feels, and feelings that go along with the golf game you desire. Make it as real and believable as possible.

5. Stick with it. A great golf game doesn't happen overnight. It takes hard work and persistence. Keep working and keep believing. See clearly the game you desire in your mind, then make it happen through practice and persistence.

Chapter 7: Cinderella Story

Filmwork

The Scene: Carl is taking a moment away from his duties as assistant greenskeeper to indulge in some daydreaming. He has an old-fashioned weed whacker in his hands, and he is using it as a golf club. As Carl fantasizes, he narrates his fantasy so the viewers are able to hear what is going on in his head. Through his narration, we learn that Carl is visualizing playing in the Masters tournament. He is doing exceptionally well, even holing out from the fairway on one occasion. As he is about to become the "Cinderella story," with "tears in his eyes," he is roused out of his dream by Bishop Pickering, who wants to play a few holes before it begins to rain.

The Quote: Carl Spackler: "What an incredible Cinderella story, this unknown comes out of nowhere to lead the pack at Augusta. He's on his final hole. He's about four hundred and fifty-five yards away. He's gonna hit about a two iron, I think. Oh, he got all of that. The crowd is standing on its feet here at Augusta. The normally reserved Augusta crowd is going wild for this young Cinderella."

> **The Lesson: Use Visualization to Improve Your Game**
> *Visualizing masterful outcomes can help you unify your mind and body in order to perform at a high skill level.*

After doing their filmwork, Pearl and Buck stayed seated in the comfortable chairs in the clubhouse lounge.

"Buck, have you ever caught yourself using visualization like Carl in Caddyshack?" Pearl asked.

"Is that what he was doing? I thought he was just daydreaming."

"Well, visualization is similar to daydreaming, and Carl's daydream seemed so vivid and real to him that I would call it visualization."

"In that case, I guess I have," Buck shrugged. "Sometimes I imagine I am Tiger Woods playing in a major or something like that." He scratched his head. "Pearl, didn't we talk about visualization in the last lesson?"

"We talked a little about visualization in our last lesson. But mostly, we talked about using visualization to give your game a big-picture goal, something to shoot for. Now, I want to talk a little more about how to use visualization to improve your skills of play."

"Okay. Now, Pearl, tell me how Carl's daydreaming counts as visualization."

Pearl obliged. "Visualization, sometimes referred to as imagery, is simply the process of generating mental pictures. Often, it involves creating a picture in *the mind's eye,* a mental snapshot or moving picture of a scene, event, or outcome. I wouldn't consider Carl's case the best I've ever seen, but it had some characteristics of a good visualization session."

"Like what?"

"First, it seemed very real to Carl. He made up a vivid story. That means his picture was very clear in his mind. It was as if he were actually at the Masters, playing his way to the championship. He could actually see himself there."

Buck's head bobbed, indicating that he was following the lesson thus far.

"Second, he made mastery images."

"Mastery? What's that?"

"Mastery means that you have perfected something or mastered it. A mastery image is visualization of a perfect outcome. Carl didn't see himself flubbing a shot, he saw himself holing out from the fairway. He didn't see himself losing the championship, he saw himself winning. It takes confidence even to imagine yourself doing something like that. So I would score that as a good feature of Carl's visualization session."

Pearl continued. "Third, Carl generated some good, strong, positive emotions during his visualization. He felt confident, relaxed, and elated throughout certain points in his session. Those are all emotions that one might use to play their best golf."

Pearl made a circular gesture with his hands. "Buck, try to wrap up into a summary everything I've told you so far."

Buck blew out a breath. "All right. Visualization, which is sometimes called imagery, is kind of like daydreaming. It's just making up pictures in your mind. Carl did a good job because he made his pictures very clear, used mastery images, and felt strong, positive emotions."

"Good, Buck," Pearl praised. "If you can remember just that, I'd be happy."

Buck raised his eyebrows. "But there's more, isn't there?"

Pearl smiled. "There's always more, Buck. There's always more."

Buck just smiled and shook his head slowly.

"Imagining yourself performing a skill can actually cause signals to be sent from the mind to the muscles used to perform that skill. In other words, your nervous system doesn't distinguish between things you actually do and things you imagine doing. Also, studies in cognitive and behavioral psychology have demonstrated the effective use of imagery for many uses including stress and anxiety reduction. Furthermore, anecdotal evidence suggests that many athletes at high levels of competition use imagery. They claim that imagery helps them prepare for and perform in competition."

"That's all great, Pearl. But can you tell me how to use it?" Buck feigned disinterest, but he enjoyed professor Pearl's little lectures.

"The overall state we are looking for when you practice imagery is for you to be relaxed and open to suggestions about your ability to play golf. Basically, you will begin the session by getting into a relaxed state, and then you will make mental pictures of how you want to play. Imagery can be that simple. Even Carl did it well."

"If he can do it, so can I," Buck said seriously. "Tell me more."

"To begin your imagery session, you need to clear your mind and relax your body, which will help us relax the mind and get into a focused state. To start, you want to get into a comfortable position either sitting or lying on your back. Breathe from the diaphragm for a minute or so to begin relaxing."

Buck closed his eyes and put his right hand on his stomach. He took a few deep breaths from the diaphragm, causing his hand to move with the swelling of his stomach.

"If you are able to achieve a good level of relaxation this way, diaphragmatic breathing may be enough for you to relax. However, you may also wish to add some progressive muscle relaxation to your breathing routine to help you relax. To progressively relax your muscles, simply tense a muscle group for several seconds, then return that muscle to a relaxed state. Begin with your feet and move your way up your body. The more muscle groups you alternately tense and relax, the more relaxed you should ultimately become."

Pearl spent a few minutes helping Buck learn the feeling of progressive muscle relaxation. He started by having Buck shrug his shoulders tightly into his neck then release the tension by having them fall back into their normal resting position. They then tried other muscle groups in the arms, torso, and legs. After doing only a few body parts, Buck began to distinguish the difference between a tense muscle group and a relaxed one.

"I think I'm getting it, Pearl. It's not hard. But is it really necessary to do all that work before doing some visualization?"

"It might not be absolutely necessarily to achieve some small benefit," Pearl started, "but it's like anything else. You get out of it what you put into it. Most people don't want to go through the trouble of relaxing before beginning imagery. I can't stress enough that relaxation is imperative to putting your body and mind in a focused and suggestible state. Without relaxing your mind and body, you won't be able to achieve the mental focus necessary to get the maximum benefit from your imagery session."

"Okay. I guess it's worth it. I promise to get relaxed. What next?"

"Once you achieve a relaxed state, you can create two basic types of images: internal and external. An internal image is one that is scene from your own point of view. In other words, internal imagery is imagery as it would be seen through your own eyes. External imagery is imagery that is seen as if it were being projected onto a screen. When using external imagery, you would see yourself through the eyes of another person.

Whether you use internal or external images is a personal preference. I recommend experimenting with both types of visualization to find which one is most comfortable for you."

"Easy enough. What should I imagine happening, Pearl?"

"You can use imagery to imagine a goal, a technique, an emotional state, the feel of muscle movement, or an outcome: the image you choose to create should be based on the goal of your imagery. If you are having trouble setting a goal for yourself, you may choose to do some imagery sessions that focus on setting goals, getting a clear picture of a specific goal. If you want to create a certain emotional state, you might want to do some imagery sessions focused on picturing yourself in the desired emotional state. For example, if you want to be confident, you might imagine yourself being extremely confident in the situations in which you desire more confidence, or you might imagine yourself in situations in which you have been confident in the past."

"So I can pretty much imagine anything I want?"

Pearl nodded his head. "Pretty much, yes. I think the best guideline for using imagery is to create as sharp a picture as possible by creating strong feelings and clear pictures. To make your pictures as clear as possible, form an image in your mind and adjust the sights, sounds, smells, feels, and tastes of the scene until they are as vivid as possible."

"Okay, Pearl. What if I am struggling with some part of my game? Can I use imagery to imagine myself getting better?"

Pearl scratched his head. "Yes. But if you are struggling with something, never imagine yourself doing something poorly. Instead, if you are going to use imagery to improve your technique, always picture a mastery image, a perfect performance of whatever technique you wish to master. Try to imagine the feel of the muscles moving in a perfect execution of your technique. This is extremely important because the brain actually sends signals to the muscles during intense imagery. If you get very good at using imagery, this is powerful information because you can use imagery to trick your mind and body into believing that you have actually performed a perfect movement even though you may have only even attempted the movement in your mind."

"Can I use visualization on the range and course, Pearl?"

"Yes, absolutely, and I encourage you to do so. You can visualize targets, such as fairways or greens, and you can visualize your shot before you make it happen. In fact, I suggest that you see each shot in your mind before you hit it. Now that you know that, you should try to incorporate visualization into your preshot routine. Before you step up to the ball, see a successful shot in your mind. Try to picture the exact shot you want to hit. It will help you become the ball. You can also visualize on the range to imagine yourself playing a particular round of golf. See it in your mind out on the range before you play it on the course."

Pearl looked at Buck, who had slumped down into the couch with his eyes closed. He looked like he might be napping or starting his first visualization session. Slowly, his lips curled into a devilish grin. He sat up and looked toward the windows that provided a view into a small courtyard where club members often enjoyed a snack and a rest. The courtyard was particularly beautiful this time of year because of the flowers that lined its borders.

"Pearl, what about using imagery like Carl did? He seemed to make visualization a lot of fun." Buck sneered with derisive laughter.

"You can also use imagery in practice to create a perfect picture of yourself in competition. Carl did this when he was chopping the heads off flowers, pretending to be the Cinderella story about to win the Masters. Obviously, Carl wasn't really at the Masters, but in his mind, he was there, playing near perfect golf. Depending on Carl's ability to focus, he may have created strong beliefs that he was actually at the Masters playing the round of his life. While imagery of the Masters is unlikely to get you into the actual tournament, you could effectively use imagery on the range to imagine yourself at a specific course. You can be creative and use as much imagery as you need to get the correct feeling. Picture yourself playing a round, choosing clubs and making shots. Or picture what it is like to feel the pressure of teeing off on the first hole, surrounded by your heckling friends. Practice in your imagery the feeling and actions of mastering the situation. When you encounter the situation in reality, you will be more likely to be successful if you believe you have mastered the situation before. Using imagery can give you this feeling of mastery without ever doing it in real life."

Buck's laughter stopped. He put a serious look on his face and cleared his throat. "So Carl did a really good job of visualization, and you would recommend I follow his lead?"

Pearl leaned forward with his elbows on his knees. He thought for a second. "Yes. I suppose so," he said after a moment of deliberation.

"Excellent. I can do that," Buck said, his eyes focused past the window.

Pearl leaned back in his chair. "Okay, Buck. How about a summary."

"Basically, you can use imagery to imagine just about anything. First you need to relax. Then you can imagine yourself doing almost anything, as long as it's a good thing. Imagine mastery images."

"Pretty good. If you can remember that, you'll be all right."

"Thanks," Buck said. Then he sprung to his feet and bolted for the door. He was almost outside before Pearl called to him.

"Buck!"

Buck stopped on a dime and turned on his heel. "Uh huh?"

"Are you going out to practice your visualization?"

"Yeah."

"Great. Have fun," Pearl said with a smile.

"Oh I'll have fun, all right," Buck thought to himself as pushed out door, intentions of emulating Carl's day at the Masters in mind. He stopped one last time when he heard Pearl call out.

"Oh, and Buck,"

"Yeah?"

"Stay out of the gardener's flowers."

Old Pearl says to remember these tips to make the most out of your visualization sessions:

1. Keep it simple. Visualization can be as easy as imagining vivid pictures of the sights, sounds, and feels of a great golf game.

2. Relax. You will benefit most from visualization if you take time to become relaxed before you start visualization. Relaxation helps the images flow and opens your mind to the possibilities created by the imagery. To begin your imagery session, get comfortable and breathe from the diaphragm for a minute or so to begin relaxing. You may also wish to add some progressive muscle relaxation to your breathing routine to help you relax. To progressively relax your muscles, simply tense a muscle group for several seconds, then return that muscle to a relaxed state. Begin with your feet and move your way up your body. If you find it impossible to relax, you may want to consult a professional (physician, psychologist, social worker, or even a message therapist) or read one of the many excellent books available on the topic.

3. Create mastery images. Always visualize yourself performing perfectly. It will help instill confidence in your game. Never imagine yourself doing something poorly. Always create mastery images.

4. Be creative with your imagery. See the images internally, from your point of view, or externally, from the view of someone else outside yourself. You can practice visualization at home, in the office, or on the range. The best guideline for using imagery is to create as sharp a picture as possible, with strong, positive feelings and clear pictures.

5. Stay out of the flowers. If you are going to imagine winning the Masters or any other tournament, do it at home, the office, or on the range. And put a golf club in your hand rather than a weed whacker

.

Chapter 8: You'll Get Nothing and Like It!

Filmwork

The Scene: The Judge and his group are grabbing a bite to eat at the turn. As they approach the snack hut, Spaulding, the Judge's slovenly grandson, is waffling about his choice for lunch. The Judge becomes perturbed with Spaulding's ambivalence and shouts one of the most famous lines in Caddyshack.

The Quote: Spaulding: "I want a hamburger, no a cheeseburger. I want a hot dog. I want a milkshake. I want potato chips....."

Judge: "Spaulding! You'll get nothing and like it!"

The Lesson: Be Decisive

Decisiveness goes hand-in-hand with confidence. In order to be confident and trust your swing, you must develop the habit of being decisive.

Pearl and Buck emerged from a canopy of trees and walked up the last few steps of a steep hill to a perfectly flat plateau that served as the 8th tee box. They stopped there and looked out at the beauty - and treachery - of their course's most difficult hole on this resplendent morning.

The 8th is a medium length par three of about 180 yards for the back tees, 160 for the front. From the tee, the land slopes steeply for about 20 yards then levels off for about the next 100 before the land gives way to a clear blue pond that reflects the morning sun with a bright glare. The oval shaped pond stretches for about thirty yards in the length of the hole. At the far end of the pond, wood planks piled on top of each other form a retaining wall for an elevated green that is three times as wide as it is deep. Tall, thick elms, especially abundant on the soft, grassy slopes around to the green, box-in the entire hole.

Pearl knew that the greatness of this hole lies not only its beauty but its tantalizing danger. The golfer about to hit to this green is presented with a stunning array of fearsome visuals. Even the most skilled golfers become a little weak-kneed and tight-fisted when facing the challenge of the 8th.

The first problem encountered is club selection and distance. The green, although elevated from the pond and surrounding land, sits well below the tee, making for a shot that requires a deceptively short club. However, lest one become too comfortable clubbing down, the course designer scooped out that beautiful blue muse of a pond in front of the green to sink any balls landing too short. Confronted with this challenge, the golfer is likely to feel more comfortable with the regular club for the yardage. On the other hand, the back of the green quickly slopes away into a thick stretch of elms that line the bank of an unseen river that flows in the distance behind the hole. Hitting past the green is not an option. Thus, the distance of the shot needs to be within ten yards of perfect. A ball hit eleven yards in front of or behind the pin is a ball drowned.

Even if the ball is hit to the perfect distance, being too far left or right of the hole is not an enviable position. The lush slopes that surround the green swallow balls whole, making extrication from the rough a difficult and risky proposition. And that's a good position to be in compared to the impossible lies that result from a slice or hook into the rows of elms that fence the entire hole.

Pearl knew Buck was fearful of the 8th. Hence the reason he chose it for this lesson. He needed a hole that forced Buck to make a choice and abandon all other options.

"What do you think of this hole, Buck?"

Buck's tension was palpable. His voiced cracked when he spoke, revealing his fear. "Well, it's a tough one. It's expensive too. I've lost a lot of balls on this hole."

"Mmmhmm," Pearl hummed. He nodded and waited patiently for Buck to elaborate, but nothing else came out of the young man's mouth. Pearl allowed the silence to linger, feeding Buck's discomfort by the second.

After a minute, Pearl reached into his pocket, bent down, and planted a ball atop a tee into the dewy grass carpet of the tee box.

Buck stared at the teed ball with mouth agape. He blinked his eyes, hoping that when he shut them the ball would disappear. But each time he opened his eyes, the ball remained. It gleamed white and bright as ever.

Pearl walked to Buck's bag, leaving him hypnotized by the ball. He pulled out three clubs: one the perfect club for the distance, one club short, and one long. He walked back and gently jabbed the clubs into Buck's ribs. Buck took the clubs without removing his gaze from the ball.

Pearl snapped his fingers in front of Buck's face. "Buck!" he barked.

Buck slowly swiveled his head to look at his teacher.

"Take me through your thoughts on how to play this hole," Pearl said low and slow.

Buck took a deep breath and slowly exhaled. "Okay, I don't want to hit it short because it would be wet. So I've got to remind myself not to hit it short."

"Go on."

"But, I don't want to be long either because then my ball will roll away down into the trees or the river."

Pearl was silent.

"I guess if I hit it left or right of the pin, but not too far left or right or short or long, it would be okay."

"If you had one thought for where you want to hit the ball, Buck, what would it be?" Pearl asked.

Buck rubbed his chin as if it would help him generate an answer. "I think because I hit it in the water so much on this hole, I would have to think, 'Don't hit it short.'"

Pearl took Buck by the arm and led him back about ten feet behind the ball. Side by side, they looked out at the hole from their vantage point behind the ball. Pearl waved his arm out in front of him gesturing for Buck to take in the entire scene.

"Buck, look at this magnificent hole. It's lush and green and blue and brown. It has water, a little bridge, a gorgeous green, sun, and shade. It's beautiful, yet when *you* look at it, all *you* can see is danger."

Buck nodded in agreement.

"When I asked you to take me through your thoughts about playing this hole you took me on a wild goose chase through all the dangerous elements of the hole. You were fearful of the danger behind and to the sides of the hole, and the water in front completely mesmerized you. You are frozen by your fear of the danger this hole presents."

Buck continued to silently agree.

"And I'm a little disappointed in you, Buck," Pearl said quietly. "But I'm also not disappointed in you."

Buck slowly shook his head. "You are? Why? I'm confused."

"Well Buck, I'm disappointed because I've already taught you how to think when you hit the ball, and you didn't even mention it when I asked you what your thoughts would be when playing this hole. Do you know what I'm talking about?"

Buck hung his head slightly. "Being the ball. I didn't think about being the ball."

"That's right. And when you become the ball, you think about where the ball *wants* to go, not where the ball *doesn't want* to go."

"I should've known," Buck said. His head slumped a little lower.

"Pick your head up, Buck," Pearl barked. "You won't make that mistake again. Besides, I brought you here for a reason. Just like almost all other golfers, your fear on this hole paralyzes your thinking. You think about all the wrong things - the dangers - and can't get your mind off of them. Your mind races on and on about the dangers, so your mind has all the dangers perfectly mapped out and marked with red X's. The problem on a hole like this is that you never tell your mind where you *want* to hit the ball. You only tell it where you *don't want* to hit the ball."

"What's wrong with that? I really don't want to hit the ball to those hazards."

Pearl tapped his temple. "The mind doesn't understand that kind of thinking. Let me explain. In golf, as in anything, it is difficult to get what you want when what you want is not clearly defined. Remember our filmwork?"

Buck indicated that he did.

"What would the Judge get Spaulding for lunch? He wants a hamburger, no a cheeseburger, a hot dog, a milkshake," Pearl threw his hands in the air. "First he wants something then he changes his mind. Then he says he wants everything. What he really wants is never clearly defined."

"Yeah, that's funny. The judge gets really mad." In his best Ted Knight voice, Buck scowled, "Spaulding, you'll get nothing and like it!" He laughed at his impersonation. Pearl did too.

When they stopped laughing, Pearl continued. "The Judge, being a ruler of the bench, has no place for indecisiveness. In his job as a judge, he surely needs to make decisions and stick by them. He has no tolerance for people who are indecisive, and his intolerance produces several of the movie's classic lines. First, he shuts down Spaulding's whining with 'You'll get nothing and like it!' Then, in no subtle terms, he lets Noonan know what he thinks about Danny's ambivalence toward college: 'Well, the world needs ditch diggers too.'"

"That's a good one too."

"A decisive mind may be one of the Judge's best attributes as a golfer. Think about some of the decisions the Judge makes and follows through on with no hesitation."

Buck looked skyward as if the answers were forthcoming via writing in the sky.

"In one scene, he kicks the ball repeatedly, stating to Noonan that 'winter rules' allow him to improve his lie."

"I remember."

"Mmmhmm. Choose to like his ethics or not, you can't deny that it takes decisiveness to cheat like that. Another good example is the final putt the Judge sinks to put himself and Dr. Beeper in position to win the match. While hunkered over the putt, the Judge decides that the putt requires the use of his special putter, 'Billy Baroo.' He replaces his regular putter and asks Spaulding to fetch him Billy. After wooing Billy with sweet talk, the Judge sinks the crucial putt. He had confidence in Billy and never wavered in the least about his decision to pull Billy out of the bag."

"That's true."

"While we generally want to avoid emulating the Judge's golf game, we would be wise to take a lesson from him in the area of decision making. A frequent downfall of many golfers is their inability to make a choice and follow through confidently on that choice. This is bad for two reasons." Pearl held up his index finger. "First, being indecisive ruins our confidence, and confidence is the key to trusting our swing and making a good shot. We can't be confident in a decision if we haven't really made a choice." He pumped his fist and his middle finger joined the index. "Second, being indecisive prevents us from having in mind a clear target. Here's why: In order to make sense of our world, the subconscious part of our brain seeks order and harmony constantly. By allowing our mind to retain opposing thoughts, we are creating disorder, and whether we are aware of it or not, our brain will automatically search for a solution to our dilemma. This unconscious search for a solution interferes with our ability to focus on our target, and therefore, we cannot become the ball and achieve mind-body unity."

"Mmmhmm," Buck hummed. His eyes stared off into the distance.

Pearl looked at him questioningly. "I lost you, didn't I?"

"Yeah," Buck admitted.

"Okay, think of it this way. If you haven't decisively picked a target or club, you can't become the ball. Your mind won't let you become the ball because it is confused about what you truly want to do."

"That I can follow."

"Indecision can creep up on us in many forms. Choosing the right club, determining yardage, reading a break, target choice, and laying up are common sources of indecision. Another common form of indecision is quite insidious. It occurs when we say to ourselves, 'Don't hit the ball in the water,' or 'Don't slice.'" Pearl cleared his throat. "Have you ever done that, Buck?"

"All the time. Anytime there is water or sand on the course," Buck said, shaking his head.

"Usually when we tell ourselves *not* to hit the ball somewhere, we fool ourselves into thinking that we are making a decision about where we want the ball to go, but really, we aren't making any decision at all. When we think in terms of *don't* and *not* we are only telling ourselves where we *don't* want to hit the ball rather than naming where we *do* want to hit the ball. Our brain is a magnificent organ, but it doesn't deal well with negative messages. It sends messages to the body much more efficiently when we simply state our goals in positive terms."

Buck nodded and looked out over the hole. He knew it would be tough to get the hazards of this hole out of his head.

Sensing his discomfort, Pearl pushed on with the lesson. "Buck, what would be a positive statement for this hole that would help you pick a target and become the ball? Keep in mind, the ball has to know where to go."

Buck scanned the hole again. "Well, I can't hit it short."

Pearl shook his head.

"I can't hit it long."

Pearl continued the shake.

"Can't hit it left or right."

"So where can you hit it?"

"I guess I have to hit this one pretty much right at the pin," Buck said.

"Mmmhmm. Good. But, I wouldn't even say 'pretty much,'" Pearl added. "I'd just say, 'Hit it right at the pin.' Do you see the difference? Pretty much is even a little vague, and on this hole, you can't afford to be vague."

"I think I'm beginning to see what you mean," Buck said.

"Here's a little more information for you, Buck," Pearl continued.

"Great," Buck said.

Pearl thought he tasted a hint of sarcasm in Buck's comment, but he continued anyway. "Actually, the brain so prefers to use affirmative statements to tell the body what to do that it will ignore *not* and *don't* statements. When you start thinking, 'Don't hit the ball in the water hazard,' the brain will ignore the 'don't' part of your statement. The resulting message that gets sent from the brain to the body is, 'Hit the ball in the water.' If you often think in terms of *not* and *don't* out on the course, your body may end up doing the opposite of what you think you told it to do, but in reality, it is doing exactly what you told it to do."

"I never thought of it that way. I guess my mind has told my body to hit the ball in the water an awful lot."

"Mmmhmm. Caddyshack even has a great scene depicting this phenomenon. In the scene, the Judge and his group are on the tee preparing to hit. The Judge is going through a horrendous preshot routine when Al Czervik yells at him," Pearl paused.

On cue, Buck replied, "I bet you slice into the woods, a hundred bucks!"

"Right. Smails, trying to be very decisive replies," Pearl paused again.

"Let me think," Buck scratched his head. "Oh yeah." Buck broke into his Judge Smails voice. "'Gambling is illegal at Bushwood, and I never slice.'"

"Very good," Pearl praised. "By using the term *never*, the Judge is producing an indecisive thought and creating confusion between his mind and body. His mind subconsciously will not recognize the "never" part of his statement and will send his body the message, "I slice." Without replacing the indecisive thought with a more decisive one, for example, 'I always hit the ball straight down the fairway,' the judge was almost certain to hit a bad shot. True to life, he struck exactly the shot his subconscious mind told him to hit. He sliced. And he owed Czervik a grand."

Buck was smiling and nodding, a good sign. Pearl felt he was beginning to grasp the lesson. "Buck, let's go to the practice range to finish this lesson."

At the practice range, Pearl pointed out several people hitting balls in rapid-fire succession. They each had a pile of balls and endlessly raked ball after ball into place, hitting them with no practice swings or mental preparation.

Pearl gestured at the frantic people swatting at golf balls. "Buck, for many people, indecision starts on the practice range. They go to the range, buy an enormous bucket of balls, and start banging them out at a breakneck pace, spraying balls every way under the sun. As we've already covered, this type of practice is not good. It results in bad mechanical habits and it does not incorporate the mental part of game into your swing. To golf excellently, we must practice excellently, and to do that, we need to include decisiveness as part of our practice."

"Are telling me that I can actually practice making decisions?" Buck asked.

"Absolutely," Pearl said emphatically. "Making decisions is a skill, and any skill can be practiced. Any time you pick a clear and specific target before you swing the club, you are making a decision. The more often you practice your decision-making skills, the more natural and automatic this skill will become."

"Hmm. I see."

"A good way to begin incorporating decision-making skills in your practice is to choose a target before each shot. You should be doing this anyway in order to become the ball. Pick a specific spot on the range to which you want to hit the ball. The spot should be rather small. If you are aiming for a green, pick a quadrant of the green as your specific target. If you are aiming down a fairway, pick a distinguishing feature of the fairway or range. If there is not a good feature in the fairway itself, many holes or ranges have trees or bunkers in the background that can be used as suitable targets."

Buck nodded away, eager to learn more.

"Another way to increase decisiveness is to increase consistency. At a moderate level of consistency, you should begin to figure out how far you hit each club. Knowing the distances you hit each club will help you choose the correct club for any given shot. Once you make the choice to go with a particular club, don't second-guess it. Focus only on the upcoming shot once you've made a club selection. Second-guessing will only result in indecision, lack of confidence, and a tentative swing."

"I'll say. That's exactly my problem on the 8th hole," Buck admitted. "I don't know which club to hit."

"The putting green is also a great place to practice being decisive. Many golfers act as if the read of a green has more interpretations than the Constitution. While it may be true that a putt struck at different speeds will react differently on the same green, you need to be more decisive when reading a putt. Choose a line and putt it. A great way to begin your putting practice is to hit in putts from very close to the hole. This will help increase your confidence and decisiveness. Start with putts that are no more than a foot or so out from the hole. Practice several from the exact same spot then move to another spot of the same distance. After consistently hitting some in the hole with confidence, move a foot or six inches out from that spot, and repeat the previous pattern of putts. Continue with this drill up to four to six feet depending on your proficiency. Remember, you want to hole about 50 to 100 percent of your shots in this drill. It is designed to increase confidence and decisiveness, and to do this you need to make the putts go in the hole. When you start to miss consistently, move back to a closer distance or change your drill."

"Anything else?"

"That should do it. If you work on those drills, you'll improve."

"Great!" Buck said. "Only......" a confused look came over Buck's face.

"Only what?" Pearl asked.

"I get the part about, 'You'll get nothing,' but I don't get the part about, 'and like it.'"

Pearl laughed. "I think the judge just meant that if you don't make a decision, you don't deserve to complain."

"Now I get it," Buck said smiling. "But I don't want to get nothing. So I'm going to start practicing making decisions and sticking with them." With those words, Buck was off in a flash toward the clubhouse.

"Are you off to play the 8th hole?" Pearl called after him.

"No! It's too expensive to learn to make decisions there. I'm going to get range balls and visualize the 8th hole out on the range," Buck called back.

Once again Pearl was pleased with his student. He was integrating lessons, which was always a good sign. And come to think of it, Pearl himself felt a twinge of intimidation standing out on the 8th tee. Maybe he should sneak off and get some practice in on the real deal. After all, even an Old Pearl needs polishing once in a while.

Old Pearl says to remember these tips when being decisive in order to avoid getting nothing and having to like it:

1. Be decisive on the golf course. Make decisions and then stick with them. Trust your decisions to be the right ones. You must have complete trust to swing the club correctly.

2. The brain deals best with positive messages. Telling yourself *where not* to hit the ball is not as effective as telling yourself *where* to hit the ball. Always choose a specific target, and once your choice is made, don't second guess it. Always send yourself positive, affirmative messages only.

3. Practice being decisive by making decisions on the practice range. Always pick a target for your shot.

4. Learn the distances you hit each of your clubs. Knowing how far you hit each club will allow you to be more confident in making decisions and trusting them.

5. Practice being decisive on the putting green. Choose a line and putt it with confidence. Don't second guess yourself. To practice this, start your putting practice very close to the hole and gradually move out to just a few feet. Being decisive on the short putts will greatly increase your consistency

Chapter 9: So I Got That Going for Me, Which is Nice

Filmwork

The Scene: Using the business end of a pitchfork, Carl Spackler has the younger D'Annunzio pinned to the wall of a barn. He is imparting some of his worldly wisdom.

The Quote: Carl to young D'Annunzio: "So I jump ship in Hong Kong, and I make my way over to Tibet. And I get on as a looper at a course over there in the Himalayas."

D'Annunzio: "A looper?"

Carl: "A looper, you know, a caddy, a looper, a jock. So I tell 'em I'm a pro jock, and who do you think they give me? The Dalai Lama himself. The twelfth son of the Lama, the flowing robes, the grace, bald, striking. So I'm on the first tee with him. I give him the driver. He hauls off and whacks one, big hitter, the Lama, long, into a 10,000-foot crevice right at the base of this glacier. Know what the Lama says?"

D'Annunzio: "No."

Carl: "Gunga galunga. Gunga, gunga lagunga. So we finish eighteen, and he's gonna stiff me. And I say, 'Hey, Lama, hey! How about a little something, you know, for the effort, you know?' And he says, 'Oh, there won't be any money, but when you die, on your deathbed, you will receive total consciousness.' So I got that going for me, which is nice."

The Lesson: Use Your Strengths

Focusing on our strengths allows us not only to utilize the best parts of our game to our greatest advantage; it also helps us generate confidence - the king of all golf-related feelings.

By the time the scene finishes, both Buck and Pearl are rolling on the floor with laughter. The scene is, after all, one of the funniest in Caddyshack, and it just gets funnier every time one sees it.

"Oh man," Pearl said. "That is one of the best scenes in Caddyshack."

"I agree. It's classic," Buck commented.

Still laughing, Pearl said, "Buck, let's do something different today. Let's begin our lesson by playing a round."

"Really?" Buck said, pleasantly surprised.

"Really, Buck. I have a lesson in mind, and I need to get some measurements. Let's go play."

Pearl and Buck headed out and played their round. They had a great time, each one having several great shots and several poor shots. Overall, Pearl was much more consistent and stayed out of major trouble. Buck had much more difficulty staying in the fairway, and he flubbed a few shots that cost him precious strokes. Throughout the entire round, Pearl made sure to ask Buck which club he was hitting for each shot. He used his golf pencil and a legal pad to record each shot he and Buck took. At the end of the round, the teacher and student headed to the range to tally up the round's play and finish their lesson.

After tallying the round, Pearl grabbed a five wood, rather than a pitchfork, and lightly tapped Buck's chest with it. He contorted his lip to resemble Carl Spackler, Bill Murray's Caddyshack character. In his best Carl voice he said, "Big hitter, the Lama, long."

Buck chuckled at the impersonation and shook his head. "Let's see what you've got, Lama."

Pearl grabbed a handful of range balls and tossed them on the ground in front of him. He took a few practice swings then stepped up to a ball. Slowly, he took back his club, then quickly and gracefully swung down at the ball, sending it in a beautiful arc straight down the middle of the range. He stepped to the second ball and repeated his actions. He then did it again a third, fourth, and fifth time. Each time, his stroke produced the same, straight, handsome arc. And, true to his word, it was a pretty long shot for an old man. Actually, it would've been a pretty long shot for a young man.

Pearl turned with his lip in the crooked, Carl-like position and looked at Buck. "So I got that going for me," he said, pausing for a moment to let it sink in, "which is nice."

Buck shook his head in silence. The old man really had some amazing golf skills.

"Buck, I've always been able to hit my 5-wood very purely. I almost never hit a bad shot with it. Every shot is just like you saw: a long, straight arc that puts me right where I want to be. I use the 5-wood everywhere: off the tee, off the fairway, from the rough, from the fairway sand, even from the fringe sometimes. I'll even swing it lightly and hit it from a shorter distance than I normally hit with the club. I can't help it. I'm just too good with the 5-wood to resist hitting it often. I've got that club going for me."

"Which is nice," Buck added.

"Exactly. I have so much confidence in that club that it is very nice to have in many situations." Pearl walked to his bag, covered his club, and slid it back into place. "So what's my point?"

Buck shrugged.

"Come on, Buck. Think," Pearl demanded.

Buck poked a divot of sod with his toe while he thought. "I guess your point is that it is nice to have a club you hit really well."

"That's pretty close. Here's what I really mean: It is so nice to have a club that I hit really well that I hit it in situations in which most people would choose another club. I choose to hit the 5-wood so much because just having the club in my hand gives me a boost of confidence, which, as we have learned, is very important when swinging the club. If I were to listen to advice from others, I would play the 5-wood less, but I would play worse. I know my game well, so I don't hesitate to use the strongest part of my game anytime I can."

Bucked kicked the divot he had been content to poke at seconds before.

"Something the matter?" Pearl asked.

71

"I don't have any part of my game that is good," Buck whined.

"Maybe not now, but the point of our lessons is that you are going to improve your game," Pearl reminded. "You need to have confidence and in the process and search for your own personal strengths. You are in a great period of your golf development, Buck. You are going to make a lot of progress very soon, and it will be very exciting for you to develop as a player. As you make progress, you'll find that you can do things you never thought possible."

Buck silently absorbed Pearl's message.

"Buck, let's take a look at how we swung 'em today."

Pearl retrieved the legal pad on which he recorded their shots for the round. Buck's breakdown went like this: Fourteen shots with the driver, two with the 3-wood, two with the 5-wood, fifteen shots with irons 3 through 9, twenty-five shots with a pitching wedge or sand wedge, and forty-one putts for a round of 99. Pearl's breakdown was: Six shots with the driver, thirteen shots with his 5-wood, fifteen shots with his 3 through 9 irons, eleven wedge shots, and thirty-one putts for a round of 76.

Buck silently absorbed the information as Pearl read it aloud.

"Buck, what do these numbers tell us?"

"That you beat me by 23 strokes," Buck said dejectedly.

"Yes, that's true," Pearl admitted, "but look deeper. What do the numbers tell us about how we played?"

Pearl handed the legal pad to Buck who read it carefully, analyzing the round's play. Buck's voiced raised in unison with his surprised eyebrows. "Hey! We used our 3 through 9 irons the exact same number of times."

"Mmhmm. What else? How about the other clubs?"

"Hmm, you putted less than me and used your driver less too. And you used way fewer wedges. I guess I chili-dipped a few shots that cost me."

"So what does that tell you?"

"If I used my wedges better, I would save a lot of strokes."

"Very true. If you became a more solid wedge player, your scores would drop dramatically. What else?"

"I need to improve my putting. That would help too."

"Yes. Putting is a big key, maybe the biggest, to scoring well." Pearl tapped the legal pad in a specific spot. "What about my five woods?"

"Yeah, I see that. You use your five woods a lot. How did you play so much better without using your driver much?"

Pearl smiled. "As I just showed you, I almost always hit a good shot with my 5-wood. I hit it more accurately than my driver, so I use it more, even though I might lose twenty or thirty yards on my first shot. Basically, I use it because I have so much confidence in it. And when I use it, my second shot is almost always from the fairway."

Buck nodded in silent reflection. "So, because you're almost always in the fairway, you hit more greens and fewer wedges from in close."

"Something like that. I am more accurate than you with all my clubs, so even if I hit my driver more, I would still come out ahead. But in my mind, I would miss more fairways with my driver, which would make me come out of the rough more, which would cause me to hit fewer greens. In turn, I would have to hit more wedges."

Buck understood Pearl's message. "So because you have your 5-wood going for you, you hit a lot of fairways and greens, which makes for fewer strokes."

"Exactly," Pearl applauded with a quiet golf-clap. "So now, what am I telling you?"

Buck volleyed with a return question. "Are you telling me I need to hit a good 5-wood?"

Pearl chuckled. "Not necessarily. I'm telling you that you need to find your own strengths. What club is going to be your magic wand, so to speak? What's going to be your strongest skill?"

Buck's eyes lit up. "Maybe driving the ball! I could be long off the tee. I could grip it and rip it."

Pearl silently mouthed the words as Buck spoke them. By now, he knew the boy's routine. "What else?"

"Maybe putting?" It came out as more of a question than an answer.

"Mmmhmm, maybe putting," Pearl nodded. "Buck, tell me how putting could be a great thing to have," he cleared his throat before imitating Carl Spackler, "going for you."

Buck removed his hat by the bill and scratched his head with his outstretched pinky. "I've always heard that you should drive for show, putt for dough. Maybe a great putting game would give me an advantage over my friends in the small bets we make. Great putting is supposed to be the key to low scores."

"Good. What else?"

"That's all I can think of," Buck said as he shook his head.

"That's because you are not thinking creatively, Buck. You're just parroting what you've heard others say. To be a great golfer, you have to use your strengths creatively. Now, if you were worse than or equal to your friends in all areas of the game except putting, how could being a strong, confident putter improve your chances of winning?"

Buck sat his hat back on his head and rubbed his face with his palms. He was really trying to think now. The hat contained the steam rising from the top of his head. "All right," he finally began, "sometimes I am just off the green, on the fringe or just short in the fairway. I never know whether to putt, chip, flop, or bump-and-run. I guess, if I were really confident in my putting game, I would always putt those shots. That would be good, because I would be more decisive and confident. Those are two things I've already learned are good for my mental golf game. Like today, I used my wedges a lot around the green, and I didn't hit them very well. Or, if I was a good wedge player, I could always be confident using my wedges around the green, and I could forget about putting from off the green or playing a bump-and-run."

Pearl smiled from ear to ear upon hearing Buck's answer. This was a real breakthrough for the young student. It showed that he'd begun to integrate the mental game lessons in a creative manner. "That's great, Buck. You are really showing a lot of promise. Now you are starting to put the lessons together and thinking creatively. Pretty soon, this will all pay off for you. Remember, it's good to hit all your clubs well, especially the putter and wedges, but having any specific strength can really give you an advantage."

Buck smiled and stared off into the distance. Pearl could see that he was playing future rounds in his mind right that minute. Slowly, Buck's smile turned into a frown.

"What's the matter?" Pearl asked.

"Pearl, how do I know what to work on? I mean, how will I know what my strength should be?"

Pearl laughed. "You don't have to decide right now, Buck. Maybe you won't know for a while. Your strength will develop out of the process of becoming a better golfer. You may not have one now, but when you get one, you'll know what it is."

"Yeah, but how will I know? Are you telling me I just will?"

"Buck, I am telling you that you just will know. You'll be able to feel it. But if you need to, chart your swings like I did here. That will give you a good idea of your strengths and weaknesses."

Buck seemed content with that answer for a moment, but again he repeated the cycle of smiling, staring off into the distance, then breaking into a puzzled frown.

"What now?"

"Pearl, what if I get so good at everything I can't decide what my biggest strength is?" Buck asked earnestly.

Pearl laughed hard this time. "Now Buck, that really is nice. If you become so good you can't tell what your greatest strength is, I'd say that is better than receiving total consciousness on your deathbed. That is really something great to have going for you. Now that is confidence."

With that, Pearl walked away, still laughing, leaving Buck on the range with a bucket of balls to find his strength. Buck just smiled and shook his head. Then he walked to his bag, took out his driver, and gripped and ripped until the bucket was empty.

Pearl's Pearls

Old Pearl says not to wait to caddy for the Dalai Lama in order to get something going for you. Remember these tips to find and develop your strengths:

1. Chart your club selection for your rounds. Try to find a pattern of strengths and weaknesses. Strengthen both areas, but be sure to play to your strengths whenever possible.

2. Relax. Finding your strengths will come naturally. You don't have to pressure yourself to find your strengths. Be patient and let them develop over time.

3. When you find your strengths, be confident in them and let them give you an advantage over your competition. Let your strengths give you great confidence in your ability to play the game excellently.

4. Incorporate your strengths into your game. If you are great with a 5-wood or long iron but erratic with your driver, hit more 5-woods or long irons off the tees. If you are great with wedges, lay up on long holes instead of always going for the green. If you're great with the putter, go after more one-putts and be confident using your putter from just off the green. If you're great with the driver, grip it and rip it!

Chapter 10: I Never Slice

Filmwork

The Scene: *As the judge and his group - including the bishop, Dr. Beeper, and Spaulding - are teeing off on the first tee, Al Czervik and his group approach the tee. Judge Smails is teeing off, taking his time with a series of gyrations and waggles in his preshot routine. Watching the judge perform his ridiculous ritual, Czervik becomes peeved and yells for the judge to hurry up. Not satisfied with the judge's response to his prompting, Czervik challenges the judge to a bet, betting that he will slice into the woods despite his lengthy preshot routine.*

The Quote: *Czervik: "I bet you slice into the woods, a hundred bucks!"*
Judge Smails: "Gambling is illegal at Bushwood, sir, and I never slice."
The judge slices into the woods.
Czervik: "Okay, you can owe me."

The Lesson: Use Self-talk and Positive Physical Responses to Communicate Positive Messages to Yourself

Self-talk is made up of the verbal messages we send ourselves when make statements about ourself or our actions. The content of our self-talk can have serious consequences for our thoughts, feelings, and behaviors. In order to perform at our best, we need to learn to talk to ourselves with positive, optimistic messages.

"Hey!" Buck said with the surprise of an enlightened Buddhist. "We already learned a little about this one. The judge wasn't being very decisive here. He was thinking, 'I never slice,' but his mind only really told his body, 'I slice.'"

Pearl handed out a compliment. "Very good, Buck. Good memory on the previous lesson. And you're exactly right. The mind doesn't work well with negative messages - messages that contain the words *not* and *never*. It

77

has trouble sending those messages to the body. Only here, we're going to use them to discuss self-talk rather than decisiveness. Do you know what self-talk is, Buck?"

Buck looked at the ground with the unstable confidence of someone who is being asked a loaded question. "Mmm, it sounds like talking to yourself, but that seems so simple it must be wrong."

Pearl nodded. "It seems simple and it is. Self-talk is simply the act of talking to yourself."

Buck frowned. "Isn't that a little weird?" he asked.

"Not at all, Buck. Many, many, normal, intelligent, and successful people talk to themselves all the time. They might even hold a sort of conversation. If done right, it can be very effective. Let me explain."

Pearl templed his fingers. "You see, Buck, we are flooded with messages about ourself all the time. Parents, family members, teachers, coaches, classmates, friends, bosses, coworkers, the media, and advertisers constantly send us messages about how good or bad we are, what we should do, what we should look like, how we should act, what we should wear, and so on. The messages are always there. Because we use these messages to form judgments or beliefs about ourselves, some of it is good and useful and some of it is not. Some of it can be downright harmful to us if we don't understand that we have the power to screen or filter these messages."

"Screen or filter these messages?"

"Yes. By screening or filtering messages I mean that at some point, we have to turn some of the messages off and listen only to certain ones. If we can't do that, we tend to get very confused and frustrated. Take this for example: Say you are golfing. On the first tee, you crush a beautiful drive 300-yards right down the center of the fairway. On the next hole, you top your tee shot and it doesn't even make it past the ladies tee."

"Uh oh, that's a....."

"Don't say it!" Pearl said quickly. "Just tell me this: After hitting those two shots, are you a good golfer, or are you a bad golfer?"

"That's easy. I'm a bad golfer. I hit a lot of bad shots."

"You see, Buck. That's filtering information. You ignored any information that might suggest you are a good golfer, and you sent yourself the message that you are a bad golfer."

"What do you mean?"

Pearl fed Buck an explanation. "You were faced with two opposing pieces of information about yourself: you hit one great shot and one terrible shot. In order to make a judgment about yourself based on that information, you had to search your memory for other examples of golf shots. Now, I know for a fact that you have hit plenty of good shots as well plenty of bad shots in your golfing lifetime. By answering that you are a bad player, I know you have filtered out the information that suggests you are a good golfer. You've only allowed the information supporting that you are a bad golfer to enter your consciousness. You see, Buck, it's like a screen door in your house. The screen lets in sunshine and heat while it keeps bugs outside. Your screen lets in memories of bad shots and filters out your memories of good shots."

Buck mentally masticated this information slowly before he spoke. "So you're saying it's a memory thing?"

"Sort of. In general, we only remember what we pay attention to. So really, the messages we filter out are filtered because we don't pay attention to them. Remember, we get information about ourselves all the time from all types of different sources. Naturally, we can only pay attention to some of it, and it's the things that get our attention that get remembered."

Buck chewed on this silently.

Pearl continued. "The great thing about attention and golf is that we can choose the events to which we give our attention. For you, Buck, you've so far chosen to give your attention to the bad shots you've hit. You not given much attention to the good shots."

Buck protested. "Yeah, but I hit lots of bad shots. I only hit a few good shots."

Pearl shook his head. "Buck, I can guarantee you that every pro on tour has hit an extremely large number of bad shots. They might not hit them now, but in their history of golfing, each one of them has hit more bad shots than you have. So they've had many more chances to remember bad shots than you have, but because they chose not to pay attention to them, the bad shots didn't stay in their memories long enough to make them think of themselves as poor golfers."

"How did they ignore all those bad shots? When I hit a bad shot, it always pops right up in my memory the next time I am in a similar situation. I can't get them out of my mind."

"I'm glad you asked. That's where self-talk comes into this whole equation. Self-talk helps us pay attention to only what we choose by focusing on and repeating messages. If we use self-talk effectively, we will repeat only useful, positive messages to ourselves, messages that make us feel confident, skillful, encouraged, energized, positively challenged, relaxed, and so forth. The words we say to ourselves have a great deal to do with our behavior."

Buck heard the word behavior and thought about sitting still and quiet in school. "What's so big about the things we say to ourselves?"

"Buck, the power of our words is awesome. What we say to ourselves affects our thoughts, feelings, and behaviors."

Buck rolled his eyes at the mention of thoughts, feelings, and behaviors. First Pearl brought up behavior and now this. It sounded like a lecture the guidance counselor once gave him.

"I know you think it sounds hokey, Buck, but if you never learn the relationship between thoughts, feelings, and behaviors, you will never truly understand why you golf the way you do, good or bad. You see, if the messages we pay attention to are bad, our thoughts will be bad, which will lead to bad feelings, which lead to bad behaviors. It goes in that order: thoughts, to feelings, to behaviors. Let's consider what happens on the golf course by working backward. On the course, what do we want our behaviors to be?"

Buck scratched his head. He wasn't exactly sure what Pearl wanted him to say. "We want to make good shots," he finally said.

"Right. And how must we feel in order to make good shots?"

Buck thought back a few lessons. "Well, I guess we want to feel confident."

"Good. Anything else?"

"Maybe relaxed?"

"Uh huh. Anything else?"

"Mmm, focused?"

"Very good. So to behave in the correct way, that is, to make good shots, we have to feel a certain way, that is, confident, relaxed, and focused. And in order to do those things, we first need to start to think in the correct way."

With the golf example in place, Buck followed this line of reasoning. "So how do we do that? How do we begin to think the correct way?" Buck asked eagerly.

"Again," Pearl said smiling, "I'm glad you asked. We're still talking about self-talk here. In order to think the correct way, we need to pay attention to the correct things, and as we learned at the beginning of this lesson, self-talk can help us do that."

Pearl cleared his throat. "Buck, I've already taught you a lot about how to think, feel, and behave. You know how to go through a preshot routine, become the ball, visualize an excellent outcome, feel confidence and trust, make choices decisively, and deal with pressure effectively. In isolation, I have the utmost confidence in your ability to do any one of these tasks, but out on the course, these things take a combination and interplay of thoughts, feelings, and behaviors. It can be difficult to put all the parts together, especially when your game is not going the way you would like. Out on the course, it's easy to let your thoughts get negative when your game takes the wrong turn. When the thoughts become negative, the feelings follow, and fear, indecision, and tension creep in and replace your confidence. When you lose the feeling of confidence, it becomes next to impossible to get the desired behavior, a good swing. In order to avoid this cycle of events, I'm going to teach you about self-talk to help you stay in control of your situation by filtering out the bad and paying attention to the good."

Buck's attention was currently fixed on Pearl's lecture.

"I'm going to give you a few simple rules for self-talk, Buck. Number one, say things that are affirmative and positive. As you already know, the mind doesn't deal well with negative messages that contain words like not and never. Instead of saying, 'I never slice,' say, 'I always hit it long and straight.' That's the affirmative part. Also, keep your messages positive. Always seek to keep yourself confident, relaxed, energized, challenged, and ready for fun. Never say anything to bring yourself down."

Pearl continued. "Second, when you make a good shot, you need to make sure you tell yourself that the good shot was due to a permanent, personal, and pervasive trait of your golf game. Tell yourself that the shot was a symptom of your good overall game, which is always good, because of the things you do right. For example, if you stick an approach right on the pin, tell yourself, 'I hit that great shot because I am a good golfer. I always golf very well because I work hard and have good mechanics and great mental focus.' We need to pay attention to the good shots and remember them. They only do us good."

"I can see where that would help."

"Third, when you hit a bad shot, you need to tell youself that the shot was not due to a permanent, personal, and pervasive part of your game. You need to talk away bad shots as things that hardly ever happen, and when they do, you can take the feedback and learn something from them. Also, sometimes you get bad breaks. They aren't really your fault.'"

Buck frowned deeply in thought.

"What is it?"

"Pearl, that sounds like excuse making, like you don't want to take responsibility for your weaknesses. How can that be good?"

Pearl nodded. "Great question, Buck. And you're right, that's what it sounds like, but there's a good reason for it. You see, as we said, we can't pay attention to everything. So if we are going to block something out of our attention, we want it to be a bad shot not a good one. Forgetting the bad ones protects our confidence by preventing a negative thought, feeling, behavior cycle. Let's take a look at an example. Say we hit a bad shot. Our natural tendency is to try to figure out why we hit the bad shot. When we think about our bad shot and our skills this way, our confidence is shaken down a notch or two. Now lacking confidence, we can't produce the desired behavior, a smooth swing and a straight shot. Instead, gripped with fear, doubt, and tension, we step up to the ball and hit a terrible shot. Now guess what?"

Buck raised his eyebrows.

"We've just triggered more negative thoughts about our skills which will lead to a downward spiraling quagmire of negative thoughts, feelings, and behaviors. As you can see, golfers need to have short memories for bad shots, and we can help ourselves forget them by explaining away bad shots as temporary, impersonal, and specific events."

Buck nodded. The point was hammered home. He now understood why so many of his games started off well and quickly fell apart. So many times he'd started a negative thought- feeling-behavior cycle by over-analyzing and criticizing his game out on the course. The solution was simple: Use self-talk to forget the bad ones and remember the good ones.

Pearl shoved his index finger into the air. "This is an important point. There is a time and place for everything. You have to realize that forgetting the bad shots is not the same as evaluating your strengths and weaknesses. During an evaluation of your weaknesses, you take a look at what you're not doing well, and you come up with and implement a plan for making those weaknesses stronger. You fix your weaknesses on the range. On the course, it is best to forget bad shots as soon as possible."

Buck could see the difference. He knew that on the course one has to protect his confidence at all costs.

"Here's the fourth point. Don't limit your self-talk to your verbal language. Body language is also an area where you can use self-talk to your advantage."

Buck took a step backward. "Huh? Talking with your body sounds a little nasty. What do you mean, Pearl?"

Pearl chuckled. "I mean that you need to have a positive physical response after each shot, no matter how bad it is."

"What's a positive physical response?" Buck wondered aloud.

"A positive physical response is an action that shows confidence, relaxation, happiness, or any other positive feeling. You see, Buck, because there is an interaction between our thoughts, feelings, and behaviors, we can help elicit the right feelings by thinking and acting the right way. If we want to be strong, confident golfers, we need to act that way. Even after a bad shot, slumping one's shoulders, hanging one's head, and pouting is no way to bolster confident feelings. A much better response would be to hold one's head high and walk confidently to the next shot, sure in your ability to make up for your last shot."

"Does that really work, Pearl?" Buck asked.

Pearl nodded emphatically. "Absolutely. In fact, some research shows that we actually will start to think and feel the way we act because of chemical changes in our body that take place with certain actions. When we smile, we feel happy. When we frown we feel sad. When we hold our heads high and move confidently, we feel confident. When we hang our heads and shuffle our feet, we feel down. It really works that way."

Buck was slowly absorbing the concept of a positive physical response. "Pearl, could you give me some examples of positive physical responses?"

"Sure. One that comes to mind is Tiger's famous fist pump. That's a positive physical response that breeds confidence and gets his game rolling. Another one from another time is Chi Chi Rodriguez's use of his club as a sword after he hits good shots. I can only imagine that the great crowd reaction to Chi Chi's antics makes him feel great, and he probably uses that feeling to stay confident for the next shot. I'm not saying that you have to have a signature move, Buck, most players don't. But you should begin to pay attention to physical responses after shots, and possibly even before the shot in the preshot routine. Begin to notice how the pros and your playing partners prepare for and react to shots. Do their actions seem to promote confidence, happiness, positive energy, and other good feelings, or do they sulk, slump, shuffle, and show other signs of negative feelings? Their reactions to their shots may have a lot to do with whether they golf well or poorly."

Buck mused, "I never thought about it that way, but I think your right about self-talk and positive physical responses. One of my friends I play with a lot always starts out playing very well. Then, sometime in his round, he always hits a really bad shot, and when he does, he starts throwing clubs, kicking the ground, and yelling negative things at himself. From that point on, his game goes down the drain. He told me he thinks he's motivating himself by yelling those things and acting that way, but after our lesson today, I think he's getting himself into a negative spiral of thoughts, feelings, and behaviors. His game is always much worse after the first bad shot than before it."

"That's a very common problem, Buck. And like your friend, most players who act that way think they are motivating themselves. But that's a poor way to motivate oneself and play golf. Positive self-talk and positive physical responses will go a long way to helping one improve their golf game."

As Buck and Pearl walked off the range, Pearl realized that he'd just given Buck a tremendous amount of new information. He felt the need to summarize the lesson succinctly.

"Buck, I understand that I gave you a lot of information, and some of it might be hard to remember. Let me give you a hint that will help you remember the main point of this lesson. A while back, I gave this same lesson to a friend of mine. Once he understood what I was trying to tell him, he helped me understand that he already did some self-talk and positive physical response work. He just didn't understand what he was doing. You see, most people have some understanding about whether the messages we send ourselves are positive or negative, and we can adjust our thoughts and behaviors accordingly if we just have a little understanding of what we are doing. For example, anytime my friend became aware that he was thinking negative thoughts, feeling negative feelings, or doing negative actions, he would ask himself, 'Is this helping my golf game or hurting it?' After asking that question, he said that he would instinctively act or think in a more positive way. Self-talk and positive physical responses were the techniques he used to help himself think and act more positively."

As they reached the clubhouse, Buck pondered Pearl's simple rule of thumb. "Is this helping my golf game or hurting it?" he quietly repeated. "Yeah, that's good. I'll use that. But if I need to remember about self-talk, I'm just going to remember Judge Smails' 'I never slice,' comment. Smails did just what he said, he just didn't understand self-talk."

Pearl says to remember these quick points to emphasize the importance of self-talk:

1. The messages we send ourselves are incredibly powerful pieces of information we use to determine our thoughts, feelings, and behaviors. The verbal and physical messages we send to ourselves during a round of golf or practice can determine how well we will play. In order to use this to our advantage, we need to harness the power of self-talk and positive physical responses to work in our favor.

2. Make your self-talk messages affirmative and positive. The mind doesn't understand negatively phrased messages that contain words like *not* and *never*. For example, instead of saying to yourself, 'I never slice,' say, 'I always hit it long and straight.' Keep your messages positive, confident, relaxed, energized, challenged, and ready for fun. Never say anything to bring yourself down.

3. Have a great memory for good shots. Remember the good ones for as long as possible. After a good shot, tell yourself that the shot was due to a permanent, personal, and pervasive trait of your golf game. Tell yourself that the shot was a symptom of your good overall game, which is always good, because of the things you do right. Pay attention to the good shots and remember them.

4. Have a poor memory for bad shots. Forget the bad ones as soon as possible. Use positive physical reponses such as holding your head and shoulders high and walking confidently to reduce the negative effect of a bad shot and begin sending yourself a positive message. Talk away bad shots as things that hardly ever happen, and when they do, they only happen because of bad breaks. Explaining away bad shots as temporary events that are not in our control and not something that can be attributed to our overall golf game helps us put the memory of the bad shot out of our mind. It protects our confidence by preventing a negative thought-feeling-behavior cycle.

5. Pay attention to the messages your playing partners and the pros on television send to themselves. How do they prepare for shots? How do they react to good and bad shots? What are the messages they are sending themselves? By being aware of the ways in which others send themselves messages, you will become more aware of your own self-communication.

6. When in doubt, rely on your own good instinct. Ask yourself, "Is this helping my game or hurting it?" You may be surprised at the power of self-communication.

Chapter 11: I'm Infallible, Young Man!

Filmwork

The Scene: Just as Carl Spackler is beginning to celebrate his fantasy storybook win at the Masters, his celebration is cut short by Bishop Pickering's attempt to squeeze in nine holes before the heavy rain starts. Carl graciously caddies for him, braving the inclement weather. As the round begins, the bishop is on fire, figuratively. His drives are divine, his approaches heavenly, his putts Godlike. He is commanding his ball to the hole in a subpar round despite howling winds and torrential rains. Just as it seems Mother Nature is going to end the round prematurely, Carl suggests that the hard stuff isn't going to come down for a few more hours, and the bishop continues play, safe in the knowledge that the good Lord wouldn't cut short the best round of his life. They push on, the Bishop continuing his righteous play in the pouring rain. Even when he misses, the beneficent winds blow his way and steer the ball into the cup. "I'm infallible, young man!" the Bishop screams as he feels the full power of the zone raging inside of him. Late in the round, the Bishop misses a crucial putt, bringing an end to his incredible run in the zone. The Bishop turns towards the heavens and curses the sky, "Rat Farts!" At the moment the words leave his mouth, a bolt of lightning hurls from the sky, smiting the Bishop, and setting him on fire, literally.

The Quote: The Bishop: "I'm infallible, young man!"

> **The Lesson: The Zone, A Place of Infallibility**
>
> *The zone is a state of being in which a player plays at or near his or her potential. It is characterized by overwhelming self-confidence, automatic and seemingly effortless performance, immersion in the present moment, freedom from worry, sharp mental focus, and feelings of complete control, fearlessness, relaxation, calmness, and enjoyment.*

Pearl shut off the television as the scene ended. He grabbed a marker and wrote on the dry-erase board mounted in the clubhouse: The zone is a state of being in which one plays at or near his or her personal best. It is characterized by confidence, control, seemingly effortless performance, focus on the task at hand in the present moment, fearlessness, relaxation, and enjoyment.

Pearl began his sermon, "Some call it the zone. Others call it the flow, in the groove, being on fire, en fuego, hot, or unconscious. It is the feeling one gets when all the breaks are going their way. For someone in the zone, it seems as if he or she can do no wrong. Every shot they take is right on the money. Their swing seems fluid and effortless. It is as if they are on automatic pilot, focused completely, fearless of negative consequences, and in total control of their game. As Bishop Pickering put it, being in the zone is like being 'infallible', incapable of making a bad shot."

Buck remained silent, knowing the sermon would continue.

"Caddyshack has two great scenes depicting the zone," Pearl said, "Carl's daydream of winning the Masters and the Bishop's immaculate round. The juxtaposition of these two scenes immerses the Caddyshack viewer in examples of the zone. First, we see Carl mentally rehearsing being in the zone as his Cinderella story comes out of nowhere to win the Masters. Second, we see on the course the Bishop physically in the zone, pulling off great shot after great shot. The scenes are comedic illustrations of the zone phenomenon, but what do we really know about it? What can empirical research tell us about this magical state of being?"

Buck shook his head. He wasn't even sure what empirical research was.

Pearl's preaching continued. "Research on the zone has found some consistent factors: overwhelming self-confidence, automatic and seemingly effortless performance, immersion in the present moment, freedom from worries, sharp mental focus, and feelings of complete control, fearlessness, relaxation, calmness, and enjoyment. This research is important because it allows us to understand that the zone is a measurable entity. It actually exists, and for those who have been in the zone on numerous occasions, the feeling of the zone is repeatable and identifiable."

Buck was a little lost. "In other words..." he prompted.

"In other words, we know how it feels to be in the zone, and we can get that feeling over and over."

Buck raised his hand and was acknowledged by a nod from Pearl. "Hold on, Pearl. Aren't we jumping the gun a little? I mean, I've never been in the zone, and I doubt if I am good enough to get into the zone anytime soon. Isn't the zone just for really good players?"

Pearl nodded. "Therein lies the rub, Buck. The only real problem with the zone is that it is elusive. It's hard to find. I have never heard a great athlete admit to being able to get into the zone on command. It isn't that simple. Most will say that they can't predict when it will happen, and it probably is true that we can't put ourselves into the zone on command. However, the zone isn't reserved for elite players. There are things even you and I can do to increase our chances of finding the zone."

Pearl paused to let his ideas sink into Buck's head.

"So you're saying that I could find the zone any day now?"

Pearl laughed. "Buck, you may or may not find the zone, but in case you do, I want you to understand what it is. And," he added with emphasis, "I want you to be able to increase your chances of finding the zone."

"How can I do that? How can I increase my chances of getting on fire?" Buck asked with renewed energy.

"Basically, you just need to practice all the things I've been teaching you. You see, Buck, the attributes of the zone simply are the basic elements of good mental golf. When we find ourselves in the zone, the mental game is in complete harmony with the physical game, which, not so coincidentally, is the basic goal of our mental game. By preparing yourself to play good mental golf, you are increasing your chances of getting into the zone. Does that make sense?"

Buck's slow nod and far off gaze meant that he was absorbing the information. Pearl needed to hammer the concept home with some connections to previous lessons.

"Let's look at a few elements of the zone and see how we can employ them in your everyday game, Buck."

"Okay. Sounds good."

Pearl cleared his throat. "First off, you have to be confident. Buck, you've done a great job working hard on our lessons and your physical mechanics, so I know you are committed to becoming a better. I know you've gone to the range and worked on your swing. You've also started to work on your mental game, honing the mental skills you will need to produce a unity between your body and mind. You are working hard at improving, and you are beginning to show some impressive improvement on the course. Even if you have a terrible round now or then, you have to believe that the law of averages is swinging to your side, and your overall game is getting much stronger. Let a feeling of confidence grow inside you, knowing that you have been working hard to improve your game. Positive results soon will follow."

"I *am* getting more confident," Buck said proudly. "Like there's this one guy I play with, and I used to always know that he would beat me when we played. And he always did. But now, I can hang with him sometimes, and I just know that I'm going to beat him one of these days."

"That's great, Buck. Here's another thing you can do to get in the zone: relax. Don't worry about upcoming shots, and let go of anger you've built up through frustration over bad shots. Golfers who tense up frequently during the round are putting their mental and physical beings in a state of tension. Neither the body nor the mind works efficiently under conditions of tension, stress, or anxiety. By relaxing, we allow the body and mind a chance to connect, so they can work together to produce an automatic, effortless swing."

"Okay. I'll try. I think my confidence will help me relax. And maybe I could work on a relaxation anchor, too. Do you think that would help, Pearl?"

"I think that would do the trick, Buck," Pearl reassured. "The third thing you can do is to trust your swing. Don't try to fix things out on the course. Remember, there are a million reasons why you might hit a bad shot, some of which are out of your control, but, hopefully, you have only been working on one correct swing. So don't over-analyze on the course. Just trust the swing you've built. Save your analysis and correction for the range. On the course, focus on the target, and trust that your muscles will do their job when your mind tells them where to put the ball. Be the ball, not the swing coach."

"Right."

"Finally, have fun. You golf because you enjoy it, right? Take in the beautiful scenery, enjoy the company of your golfing partners, and hit a few good shots. Forget the bad shots. Golf is meant to be fun. Take advantage of your time on the course and have a good time."

"I can do that. I love to golf," Buck beamed.

"I know you do, Buck, and by working on the individual elements of good mental golf - being confident, relaxing, trusting your swing, and having fun - you are working on elements of the zone over which you have some control. Practicing these elements and using them on the course will help you unify your body and mind to begin your round. A few good shots might be enough to transcend you to the magical state of being known as the zone."

A frown suddenly crossed Buck's face. "Pearl, is that it? Is that all I have to know about the zone?" he asked, suddenly intensely curious.

"I think so," Pearl responded. "Remember, it's best not to over-analyze the zone. Keeping it simple is the best plan."

"Yeah, but what if I find myself in the zone? I might freak out and get myself right out of it," Buck shrieked, feeling a little freaked out at the moment. He pleaded for more answers. "How do I stay in the zone once I get there?"

Pearl laughed hard at Buck's sudden, frantic worry. "What if we are lucky enough to find ourselves in the zone, huh? How do we take the most advantage of this optimal state of mind-body unity? How can we hope to harness the power of the zone and use it to our advantage? Is that what you're getting at?"

Buck nodded furiously. "Yeah, if I get there, I want to stay there. How do I stay in the zone?"

"Okay, Buck. It seems you are right. I left out some important information. Basically, you stay in the zone the same way you found it. The first thing you can do is to realize that you have done something right to put yourself into a position to get into the zone. Golfers who are thinking negative thoughts, over-analyzing their swings, or not trusting their swings will not suddenly find themselves in the zone, effortlessly hitting great shots, nor will they stay in the zone if they were there in the first place. The zone is reserved for players who have a relatively high level of confidence in their swing. That does not exclude beginners or hacks from finding the zone from time to time. They simply are unlikely to find it when they are not doing things right mentally. For a golfer to find the zone, it is a prerequisite to have confidence in one's swing. If you happen to find yourself in the zone, let your confidence surge with the knowledge that you deserve to be in the zone because you have been practicing hard and doing certain things very well."

"Okay, what else?" Buck demanded.

"Stop thinking so much!" Pearl shouted. It was more of a command than an emphasis of a previous lesson. "Do not over-think the situation by analyzing your swing mechanics, calculating your scores for holes you have yet to play, theorizing about what you did to get into the zone, or trying to figure out how long the zone will last. Just enjoy the moment. Free your mind to focus on the target and let things happen – trust your muscles to do their work correctly. Be the ball."

"All right, anything else?" Buck said in a mildly calmer tone.

"Yes," Pearl said softly. "Relax. There shouldn't be any pressure to do anything great. The zone might help you shoot your best round ever, or it might just help you drop a shot or two. A momentary zone might only help you make up for a lousy beginning or end to round. The end result doesn't matter. What matters is that you take advantage of the zone as it occurs, and to do this, you must relax. You got into the zone by being relaxed rather than tense, so continue to relax and play a good mental game."

He continued. "Remember this: The zone really is just a natural extension of a sound mental golf game. If you are doing things right, the things you've learned in our lessons, you'll probably find the zone from time to time. Don't put pressure on yourself to get into the zone, just do things right and relax. Putting pressure on yourself will only prevent you from finding the state of relaxation and trust needed to get into the zone. Go out and have fun. Trust your swing. Be confident. And finally, try not to curse the higher power when your time in the zone comes to an end - especially in a thunderstorm."

Pearl's Pearls: Pearl says to remember these tips to play in the zone:

1. The zone is a culmination of all the components of your mental and physical game working in harmony. Work on your complete mental golf game. Practice each principle of the mental game and build a physical set-up and swing that you can trust.

2. Be confident. Begin in practice, through repetition and performance accomplishment, and take your feelings of confidence to the course. Store the great shots in your memory and forget the bad ones. Be confident that your efforts to improve your game are going to pay off now.

3. Mentally and physically relax. It is a prerequisite to getting in the zone. If you find it impossible to relax, seek out help from a professional (psychologist, social worker, medical doctor, etc.) or a book on relaxation.

4. Trust your swing. It will do you no good to try to analyze which one or two out of a million things could've gone wrong with your shot. Concentrate on the one correct way you know how to swing and visualize a perfect shot before each swing. Then focus on the target, become the ball, and swing.

5. Have fun. It should be the reason you play the game. Enjoy your surroundings, company, and time.

Chapter 12: Noonan!

Filmwork

The Scene: *Danny Noonan needs to sink a putt to win the Caddy Tournament. To the winner of the tournament goes a beautiful second-hand trophy and a strong recommendation for the Caddy Scholarship. A large, rowdy crowd has assembled around the 18th green to see the outcome of the match, and undoubtedly, to cash in on side bets they have made with each other. Without the aid of tournament marshals, nobody has bothered to post polite "Quiet Please" signs, and Bushwood Country Club is quickly becoming home to some bush-league tactics. Some of those who have bet against Noonan decide to improve their chances of winning by heckling him. Chants of "Noonan!" and snarls of "Miss it Noonan," can be heard from the raucous gallery. Calmly, Noonan takes his position over the putt and blocks out all the distractions. He then rolls a putt into the cup to win the Bushwood Caddy Tournament.*

The Quote: *Hisses from the raucous gallery: "Miss it, Noonan. Miss it. Noonan!"*

The Lesson: Learn to Deal with Pressure

At some point, all golfers feel pressure to perform. Being prepared for that moment is the key to handling it well. A good preshot routine and an anchor can go a long way to prevent caving under pressure, or choking. Remember this, for everyone who is tense, anxious, or worried about screwing up, there may be someone equally tense, anxious, or worried about them playing well. If you find yourself feeling pressure, focus on the pressure your opponent is feeling.

After watching the film clip, Buck followed Pearl to the practice green. On the green, Pearl set up a putting drill and began to putt. Pearl was putting from about 5 feet away from the cup. He had a mound of balls several feet away from his putting spot, which was marked with a ball marker. After each putt, Pearl walked a few feet to retrieve a ball then spotted the ball just in front of his marker. Next, he carefully lined up his feet and shoulders. After achieving proper alignment, Pearl stared at the cup for a few seconds then made three deliberate practice strokes. Next, he stepped up to ball, aligned his feet, shoulders, and putter, and stared at the cup for about two seconds. Finally, he slowly tracked his gaze back to the ball and made his stroke. He rarely missed, and when he did, he missed by only inches, leaving an easy tap in putt.

Pearl putted about twenty balls during his drill. In the process, the forced patience nearly drove Buck to the brink of insanity, but he was determined to watch and learn. Finally, Pearl set his putter against his bag and addressed Buck.

"Learn anything interesting?" Pearl wondered.

"I noticed you did the same thing every time. It was like.....clockwork," Buck observed.

"Very good observation. I'm glad you noticed. Our lesson today is about hitting shots under pressure." Pearl walked to his mound of balls and placed one just in front of his marker. "It looks easy, doesn't it?" He asked Buck.

"It did look pretty easy. Even I can make five footers," Buck said proudly.

"Really?" Pearl looked surprised. He posed a question. "Maybe this practice putt is easy, but would it be easy if something were riding on the putt?"

Buck knew the old man was setting a trap, but he was game for anything. Attempting to capitalize on a previous lesson, Buck decided to be confident. "That five foot putt would still be easy," he said with a hint of arrogance.

Pearl smiled a devilish grin and walked over to his mound of balatas. He picked one up and placed it just in front of his mark. "Here you go, Buck. Sink it and win a dollar."

Buck almost fell over laughing. The old man thought a dollar would get him fired up. He stepped up to the ball and confidently stroked it into the cup. Buck held out his hand. "You owe Buck a buck," he said, referring to himself in the third person.

"Fair enough," Pearl said, fishing a crumpled bill out of his wallet. "Try again."

Buck set up a ball in front of the marker. He stepped up to it and eyed the cup.

"Sink it and win twenty bucks," Pearl said as Buck was about to hit the shot.

Buck stopped and looked at Pearl. The man was serious. Choosing to take Pearl's money, Buck re-aligned himself. He took another look at the cup. He thought about the twenty dollars.

"Miss it and lose twenty," Pearl added sternly.

"Huh?" Buck muttered. He looked up from his putt.

"It's only fair, Buck." Pearl said, feigning innocence. "I even gave you a chance to go a buck up. Now you just have to make the same easy putt you just made, and you will win twenty bucks. What could be easier?"

"But if I miss, I'll lose twenty bucks," Buck protested mildly.

"But if you make it you'll win twenty," Pearl pointed out. "It's an easy putt. You said so yourself."

"But it's not easy if there's twenty bucks riding on it," Buck protested moderately.

"What makes it not easy? It's the same putt."

"It's not the same putt if twenty bucks is at stake!" Buck protested vehemently.

"You're pretty worked up. You better putt now before you get really upset."

Buck shook his head. He was fuming at Pearl for messing with him. Besides being mad at Pearl, he was worried about losing twenty bucks. He tried to compose himself, stepping back to read the putt, but it did no good. He could only focus on the twenty-dollar bet he had with Pearl. He thought about losing the money and being short twenty bucks. Then he became even more irritated when he thought about Pearl pocketing his winnings. Buck's palms were sweating and shaking a little. He wiped them on his shorts then tried to steady them on the grip of the putter. He looked at the hole, tried to focus on it, but remained fixated on the thought of the bet. Finally, convinced for a moment that it was an easy putt, he made his stroke. From the moment he moved his putter into the backswing, he knew he had missed. He pushed the ball three feet past the cup.

"Looks like this lesson will cost you twenty dollars," Pearl said.

Pearl's words struck Buck with a bitter flavor. "It better be worth twenty," he mumbled to himself as he handed Pearl a ten and two fives.

Pearl began his first paid lesson. "Unlike our friend, Mr. Noonan, most of us play with enough etiquette that we don't have to deal with hecklers. Although, I'm sure some of us have friends who aren't above those types of tactics. The point is, we all have distractions that come to mind when we are about to make a swing or putt. We might be distracted by a celebrating group on another green, the thought of our last terrible shot, the excitement or disgust we feel at how we are playing, a noise one of our playing partners makes, the pressure of a big shot, or any other of the millions of thoughts or feelings that might present themselves as we are about to swing the club."

"Like being worried about losing twenty bucks?"

"Yes, like being worried about a bet. The point is, when we get distracted, we tend to start thinking, and as we know from a previous lesson, thinking too much is to be avoided."

Buck nodded in agreement.

"Actually, it's not even thinking we need to avoid. We need to avoid *distracted thinking* - thinking about things that aren't going to help us make the shot. That's the key."

Buck had the confused puppy look.

Pearl tried to clarify his message. "Usually, when we get distracted, we get nervous or frustrated, and we forget the fundamentals of our shot. For example, Buck, what were you thinking about when you were trying to sink the putt for twenty dollars?"

"Twenty dollars," Buck said plainly.

"Yes, I'm sure you were thinking about the money, but were you focused on the money, or were a number of thoughts running through your head?"

"I guess I was thinking a lot of things," Buck said. "I was mad at you, and I was worried about losing twenty dollars. I got nervous. Then I tried to focus, but I kept thinking about those other things. It was hard to focus."

"That's exactly what happens to a lot of us when we face a pressure situation. We start thinking about many, many things that are going through our heads at the moment, and we don't know how to turn those thoughts off," Pearl explained.

"Yeah, that's what happened to me. I couldn't stop thinking all those other thoughts. I tried to focus but I couldn't."

"Buck, what do you think is the best way to turn off those other thoughts so you can focus?"

"If I knew, I would be twenty dollars richer," Buck quipped.

"True, true. But what have we already learned? What is a good technique that helps us focus for the next shot?"

Buck searched his memory for lessons. "While we're young!" He shouted. "We learned that a good preshot routine can help us focus for the next shot."

"Very good," Pearl praised. "People who are affected most by pressure have poor preshot routines. They can't turn off those distracting thoughts because they don't have a script for turning on helpful thoughts. A good preshot routine can give you a script to follow to put helpful thoughts in your mind's focus. If you find yourself distracted and not following your preshot script, all you have to do is take a step back, recall your preshot script, and follow it."

"That makes sense," Buck agreed. "That was one of my problems. I was trying to be confident, but when I couldn't seem to find that confident feeling, I didn't know where to turn. I was lost."

"Right," Pearl said. "When you are lost and thinking about too many distractions that are putting pressure on you, you need to know what to think about. You need an anchor to hold onto."

"An anchor? Like the anchor you told me about when we did the lesson on confidence?"

"One in the same. All you have to do is fire the anchor. But remember, it helps to do work on the anchor. Really drill it in so that you can fire it easily whenever you need it. In that way, you have to prepare to be confident and block out distractions far in advance of the actual pressure situation. You have to be prepared, Buck. What you put in is what you'll get out. If you practice and prepare well, you'll be more confident and less distractible."

"Okay, I can do that. So the confidence anchor I am already working on can help me avoid being distracted. That's cool. It's like two tricks in one. What else can I do to avoid distractions, Pearl?"

"Well, I think having a good preshot routine that puts you in a good physical and mental set-up is the best thing. An anchor is good too. But I have one other trick that has worked well for me. It can even help you become a little calmer when you lose focus and get nervous."

Buck was in rapt attention to Pearl's words. "Let me hear it. I'm all ears," he said eagerly.

"I call it the focus flip," Pearl said, making a rolling gesture with his hands.

"The focus flip? How does it work?"

Pearl thrust his index finger in the air as a gesture for Buck to wait a minute. He then grabbed a ball from the pile he was using for his putting drill and set it about four feet from the cup. He made sure to set it on a small crest of green so that there would be a little break in the putt.

"Here's a little putt that's not too easy but not too tough either. Would you be nervous if you had to make this putt for money or to win a tournament?"

Buck nodded. "I think I would. I guess it would depend a little on how much was riding on it."

Pearl dig into his pocket and brought out his wallet. He pulled a one hundred dollar bill from his pocket. "Let's say a hundred is riding on this putt. Would you be nervous then?"

Buck nodded vigorously.

"Let's see." Pearl took Buck by the arm and led him into position by the ball. "Now, pretend we are betting a hundred on this putt. Imagine what you would start feeling and thinking."

Buck took a few practice swings. "I'm a little nervous going through my preshot routine even though no money is on the line."

"Who said there's no money on the line?" Pearl asked.

Buck was confused. "You did. You said we were pretending, just visualizing."

"Well, I lied," Pearl said matter-of-factly. "I've been giving you free lessons. Now's my chance to get some remuneration for my efforts. This putt is for a hundred dollars. You can pay me in installments if you need to."

Buck was stunned. He had to make this putt, or he would owe Pearl a hundred dollars. The cup that once looked the normal size looked as tiny as a thimble. His hands trembled a little and his palms began to sweat. He tried to go through his preshot routine, but the thought of losing a hundred dollars over this little putt was already eating away at him. He couldn't turn off the nervous energy and thoughts about how hard this little putt could be.

Pearl could see that Buck was getting nervous. He'd already gone through his preshot routine twice and his hands were unsteady. "Okay, Buck. Let's change this up. Move over, and I'll putt for the hundred."

"Huh?"

"Change places with me. I'm going to putt for the hundred while you watch."

Buck slowly and reluctantly moved back. He watched Pearl step confidently into place and begin his preshot routine. Then Pearl stepped up to the ball and with his eyes traced his line back from whole. Just as

Pearl started his backswing, he stopped it in midswing and turned to look at Buck.

"Nervous?"

"Yeah. I'm more nervous now that you're putting than I was when I was putting. You're definitely going to make this easy putt."

Pearl smiled. "Oh, you mean that you can be nervous watching somebody putt, too?"

"I bet I'm more nervous than you are."

Pearl smiled and stroked the putt smoothly into the center of the cup. "Thanks for teaching the focus flip lesson, Buck."

"Ah, you're welcome, but what did I do?" Buck asked, confused.

"You showed me all about the focus flip," Pearl praised.

"How did I do that?"

"Simple. Were you nervous when you thought you were putting for a hundred dollars?"

"Yeah."

"I wasn't when I was going to putt. Do you know why?"

Buck shook his head slowly. "Maybe because you know you're good at putting."

"No. I probably would miss that putt about as many times out of ten as you would. I wasn't nervous because just before I started my preshot routine, I took a few seconds to focus on how nervous I imagined you to be. You being nervous about the putt was kind of amusing and funny to me. It put me at ease, so I was able to step up to the ball and stay calm."

Buck noodled with this idea for a moment. "You mean, you stayed calm by thinking about how nervous I was while watching you putt?"

"That's right. You know Buck, for every person who gets nervous about missing a big putt or shot, there is another person who is nervous that they are going to hit it well. That's the idea behind the focus flip. You just need to shift perspective and look at the putt from somebody else's point of view. Imagine how nervous they are that you are going to make a putt or good shot. That should put your mind at ease and let you be more confident. You should still rely on your preshot routines and any anchors for the situation, but the focus flip can get you out of a jam if you find yourself getting nervous and not being able to focus."

"I never thought of it that way," Buck mused.

"I know, Buck. With the focus flip, preshot routine, and an anchor, you should be able to stay calm under pressure."

"Yeah, I think it will help me," Buck said as he walked toward the mound of balls.

"Where are you headed?" Pearl asked.

"To get prepared. I need to practice my anchor and preshot routine so I can stay calm and focused under pressure."

Pearl smiled and nodded. The student was going to practice. He should've known. "Buck, one more thing," Pearl called to him.

"Yeah?"

"What happened to Danny Noonan after getting heckled?"

Buck paused and searched his memory storage for the answer. A wide smile crossed his face. "He made his putt."

"That's right. And you will too. Just be prepared."

Pearl's Pearls: Old Pearl says to remember these tips to perform confidently under pressure:

1. Distractions come in all forms: intrusive, distracted thoughts, noise from others on the course, a loud mower, a side bet, an important shot, a heckling playing partner, and the list goes on. To focus, rely on the fundamentals. Set yourself up in a good stance and position, work through your preshot routine, and become the ball.

2. Remember: the best defense against choking under pressure is to be prepared. Have a good, solid preshot routine that gives you confidence. The preshot routine is your script for every shot. Don't deviate from it under pressure. The preshot routine will help you remember that your upcoming shot is just like thousands of others you've made.

3. Develop an anchor to help yourself feel confident and then practice it often. Being able to fire an anchor easily and effectively is a great defense against pressure. (Once again, here's the way to anchor a feeling: To anchor the feeling of confidence or any other feeling you want to have, recall some of your good shots that make you experience the desired feelings. Next, focus on feeling that feeling as strongly as you can. Let the feeling build in intensity. To anchor the feeling, do something or say something that you can easily repeat on the course while continuing to feel the feeling within you. Practice this a few times a day, and soon you'll be able to become confident just by triggering your anchor.)

4. Use the focus flip to reduce your nervous energy. If you find yourself becoming nervous about hitting a bad shot, put yourself in someone else's shoes and imagine that they are nervous that you are going to hit a good shot. Project your nervousness onto them, then start your preshot routine.

5. Remember Noonan! He made his shot.

Chapter 13: A Man Worthwhile

Filmwork

The Scene: The judge has gathered friends and family on the dock of the Rolling Lakes Yacht Club to christen his new sleuth, aptly titled, The Flying WASP. Before his wife, pet-named Pooky, can anoint the vessel with a bottle of champagne, the judge addresses the esteemed assemblage with a poem he has written.

The Quote: Judge Smails: It's easy to grin, when your ship comes in, and you've got the stock market beat; but a man worthwhile, is the man who can smile, when his shorts are too tight in the seat.

> **The Lesson: Keep a Good Mental State Even When Things Are Going Against You**
>
> *Golf is a game that is very easy to love when the breaks are going one's way. However, golf is a game that is difficult to play at a consistent level, and frequently, one will play at a level below their potential for many weeks or months. When slumps occur, it is a man (or woman) worthwhile who can rise above his (or her) slumping play and love the challenge that golf presents. At its essence, golf is a game that pits a player against neither his score nor the course but against himself.*

"Buck," Pearl said sharply out on the first tee, "do you think you would shoot a better score if you were able to put every tee shot in the fairway or on the green?"

Buck nodded confidently. "Absolutely. That's one of my biggest problems. I just know that if I could get everything in the fairway to start each hole, I'd play a lot better. That seems like one of the keys for you, and I'd like to play just like that."

"Have you ever had a round where that happened?"

Buck rubbed his chin with the back of his hand. "Just last week I played a round where I hit a lot more fairways than usual."

"And how'd you score?"

"I shot my best round ever, 88," Buck said proudly.

Pearl was impressed. "Congratulations, Buck. That's great. I bet when you were hitting those fairways, you were filled with confidence, weren't you?"

"I really had a great feeling of confidence throughout the whole round. I think it was one of the things that really helped me. I mean, I have my preshot routine, my anchors, and my self-talk to help my confidence, but it just seems to come so easily when I get off the tee well."

"That's outstanding, Buck. I hope you have many more rounds like that in your future. There's a catch, though."

"A catch? What do you mean, Pearl?" Buck asked, genuinely curious.

"Well Buck, you're not always going to get off the tee well, and somehow, you have to fight through it. You have to learn to play a good game even when it seems your game is going down the drain. Are you ready for that challenge?"

Buck thought about Pearl's proposition. "I guess I'm ready. I mean, if that's what I need to do to get better."

"It is." Pearl said definitively. "Here's the thing, Buck. It's just like our filmwork today. It's easy to love golf when all the breaks are going your way, but the best golfers, the golfers worthwhile, love the challenge of playing through adversity. Do you know what I mean when I say adversity, Buck?"

"Not really," Buck admitted. "It doesn't sound like a good thing, though."

"Adversity is any kind of hardship or misfortune. For example, some common adversities in golf include bad bounces, bad weather, distractions from playing partners or a gallery, poor course conditions or grooming, and a player's physical health. Probably the most common adversities experienced in golf are the minor imperfections that creep into one's swing and cause the ball to go off course. A major portion of any good golfer's existence is spent trying to perfect a swing and then correcting the minor flaws that tend to surface from time to time. You see Buck, there are many challenges in golf: playing against partners, the course, a low score, and so on. But the greatest challenge in golf is playing against oneself, battling one's negative thoughts, conquering one's tendency to swing imperfectly, and maintaining a positive, productive outlook."

"Pearl, I think I understand the challenge of golf. It's a difficult game," Buck chimed in.

"That's all well and good, Buck." Pearl cleared his throat as if to make his next statement as crystal clear as possible. "Here's the distinction I want you to understand. Anyone can accept and understand the challenges of golf, but when one can smile and *embrace* all the challenges that golf presents, then one truly has the mindset to become a great golfer. That is the challenge I've set in front of you. You need to do more than understand the challenge. You need to *love* and *embrace* the challenge of playing against yourself and your natural tendency to play at less than your best. When you do that, golf will be transcended into more than a sport. It will become a metaphor for life."

Buck silently absorbed Pearl's words. He wasn't totally sure about what Pearl was saying, but he got the gist. There is more to golf than just a score on a certain course. Golf is really about the challenge of performing and thinking one's best under any conditions, two things that matter in life as much as they matter on the golf course. And in golf, as in life, things can get tough. As Judge Smails says, it's the man worthwhile who can take the bad with the good and make the most of it.

Pearl started walking down the fairway. "Follow me, Buck."

Buck responded from the tee box. "Pearl, you said I was going to play today. Don't I have to tee off?"

Pearl stopped and turned on his heel to face Buck. "No," he said crisply. "Today's lesson is about learning to love the challenge of overcoming adversity. Today, I'm going to give you your tee shots."

Buck hustled to follow Pearl, who was heading for a thick stretch of maple trees down the right side of the hole. As Pearl reached the first trees, he drop kicked a ball into their shade. When Buck caught up with him, Pearl stood next to a ball nestled deep in the rough behind a tall maple tree. Buck understood that the ball represented his first tee shot.

"Here's the game today, Buck. I'm going to give you your tee shot on each hole. None of them are going to be very good. Your challenge is to rise above the adversity of a bad tee shot and play your best. If you can do that, I'll know you are ready to take on the challenge of becoming a great golfer."

For the next four hours, Pearl did everything he could to make Buck's second shots difficult. He placed Buck's tee shots behind trees, in thick rough, and in the sand. He even gave Buck a penalty stroke for hitting into a water hazard off the imaginary tee and made him hit his third shot from the rough on the far side of the hazard. For his part, Buck chipped, punched, and pitched his way out of trouble, plucking himself out of one bad tee shot after the next. He was decisive and calm under pressure. He used his preshot routine, anchors, focus on the target, confidence, visualization, and self-talk to maintain a great mental state for golf. When the round was finished, Buck had shot a 90, just two strokes behind his best score ever.

Pearl held out the scorecard for Buck to examine. His eyes grew huge when he noticed his final score.

"A 90?" he said with equal disbelief and exclamation. "I shot a 90?"

"That's right," Pearl said smiling. "Just two strokes off your best score ever. And you did it with 18 terrible tee shots."

"I can't believe I scored that well."

"Well believe it," Pearl instructed. "And you did it because you were up to the challenge. Buck, if you would've shot those tee shots on your own, your head would've been so filled with negative thoughts that it would have been very difficult to focus on a good mental golf game. But when presented as a challenge, you rose to the occasion and played a great round.'

Buck beamed with pride.

"And do you know what? You could've shot that 90 even if you had shot that badly off the tee. You truly have it in you to overcome adversity." Pearl patted Buck on the back. "I bet you learned something new about yourself today, didn't you?"

"I sure did. I would've never thought that I was capable of shooting that well after having eighteen bad tee shots. But I never worried about how bad those tee shots were. I was just focused on playing a great second shot. It never occurred to me to worry about how bad my tee shot was and the bad position it put me in."

"It was your ability to welcome the challenge of playing from bad lies that enabled you to focus on your second shot and play good golf despite the bad tee shot positions," Pearl informed. "If one were to actually shoot those eighteen poor tee shots, most players would reject the challenge of playing well despite adversity, and they would give in to a negative cycle of thoughts, feelings, and behaviors that would result in a terrible outcome for their round. But you were able to ward off the negative cycle. By embracing the challenge of playing to your best despite adversity, you put yourself in a great mindset, and you were able to put your mental skills to effective use."

Buck agreed. "That's seems about right."

"You see, Buck, now you know you have it in you to play well despite bad breaks and bad shots. I don't think I could've made this round harder for you, and you played to within two strokes of your all-time best score. Job well done. You really are ready for the challenge of becoming a great golfer. You are a man worthwhile indeed."

Buck was on cloud nine. He could feel a change coming over him. He had done something on the golf course that he had never done before - overcome terrible tee shots. He knew from his lessons that his confidence was growing as a result of what Pearl called *performance accomplishment*.

Amid his basking in glory over his round, Buck had a sudden burning question. "Hey Pearl, what did you mean about golf being a metaphor for life?"

Pearl templed his fingers and rubbed his fingertips against one another. "Buck, remember this: If golf was easy and we always played well, golf wouldn't be any fun. Think about it. Why don't we make a sport out of dropping pebbles in a bucket? It's just too easy, that's why. There's no challenge. But with golf, we have all the challenge we need and then some. That's why golf is so much fun. It's the challenge that makes it a great sport. A lot of people forget that and become discouraged. They think that golf is a battle against the course or against a score, but that's not the case. Always remember that golf is a battle against yourself and your tendency to settle for less than your best. That challenge never goes away, even when you're playing well."

"Where does life come in?"

"Life, like golf, is filled with challenges that appear to be external, but are internal in reality. For example, we feel that things like success in school, jobs, and or paying the bills is based on someone else's expectations for us. But in reality, those challenges are really about our ability to search within ourselves for the solutions to the problems before us. Sometimes it's an idea, sometimes it's a behavior, sometimes it's just plain persistence, but our ability to meet the challenges we accept determines our success in life. Sometimes things go well. Everyone can deal with those situations. But in life, our success is often determined by how we deal with adversity. And to deal with adversity, we have to learn to embrace the challenges before us, otherwise, we'll shrink away from the challenge and never overcome it. If golf teaches you nothing else, Buck, let it be this: The specific challenges and goals might be different in golf and life, but the process of learning to love the challenge is the same. The person worthwhile is the person who can take a step back from adversity, see that it's an inevitable part of life and sport, and enjoy the process of working through adversity to achieve a goal."

With those words, Pearl walked away and left Buck alone to contemplate the larger meaning of golf. Although Buck didn't always understand the words Pearl used, somehow he intuitively understood the old man's message. At its simplest form, golf was about what Buck would call *attitude*, and one's attitude toward golf was likely to be similar to one's attitude toward life. By learning about one's attitude toward golf, one might learn about his attitude for life. And like Judge Smails's quote, Buck felt that the man worthwhile was one who could smile when things weren't going his way. That was the key to success in golf - and possibly life too.

Buck smiled to himself as he walked off the course. He was improving and he knew it.

Pearl says to remember these keys to smiling when your shorts are too tight in the seat (so to speak):

1. Golf would be no fun if everyone were good all the time. Our bouts to overcome poor play are what make golf so much fun. Remember, golf is about embracing the challenge of overcoming our tendency to settle for less than our best. It is an internal pursuit that is as applicable to life as it is to golf. Enjoy the challenge and the excitement it brings to life.

2. Golf is about embracing challenges. In golf, the challenges are often concrete (scores, courses, etc.), although the biggest challenges, the internal challenges against ourselves, are often more ambiguous. They are similar to challenges we face in life. In this way, golf can be a metaphor for life. If we look deeply enough, we may find that improvement in golf is a metaphor for improvement in life.

3. Take the poor tee shot challenge that Buck took. It will test your ability to maintain a positive mental state and employ your mental game skills.

4. Remember to *smile when your shorts are too tight in the seat*. It will go a long way to helping you overcome whatever obstacles you face.

Chapter 14: You Ain't Gettin' No Coke

Filmwork

The Scene: *Danny Noonan has been left by Lou, the caddy manager, to attend to the Caddyshack while Lou is out for a while. A tired and weary D'Annunzio comes to the Shack to get paid and have a beverage. When Noonan charges D'Annunzio exorbitant fees for a Coke, D'Annunzio's temper flares and a fracas ensues.*

The Quote: *Noonan: "I can't pay you. Lou has to."*

D'Annunzio: "Where is he?"

Noonan: "He's out."

D'Annunzio: "I can see that he's out, Numbnuts. Gimme a Coke."

Noonan: "One coke."

D'Annunzio: "Hey, wait a minute! That's only fifty cents!"

Noonan: "Yeah, Lou raised the price of Coke. He's been losing at the track."

D'Annunzio: "Uh-hoh! Well I ain't payin' fifty cents for no Coke!"

Noonan: "Uh-hoh! Then you ain't gettin' no Coke. Know what I'm talkin' about?"

The Lesson: You'll Get out of Golf What You Put into It

Many people become frustrated with golf because they erroneously think that golf is about a final score rather than a process of continual improvement and setbacks. Ultimately, we will get out of golf what we put into it. There are no shortcuts. In Caddyshack-speak, we cannot get the Coke if we have not paid the appropriate price. Conversely, if we are willing to pay the asking price, all the Coke we desire is ours for the taking.

113

The morning of Pearl and Buck's final lesson was clear and beautiful. The air was warm and the sky was brilliant blue. The smell of freshly cut grass invited them to play. It was the type of morning when the very air around them seemed filled with energy and optimistic promise.

Teeing off on the second hole Pearl began the lesson. "Buck, most bad golfers make a common mistake. They go down the wrong path so to speak. I want to tell you about that mistake, but I want you to learn something more. Rather than just learning about the common mistake, I want you to learn how to travel the correct path."

"Okay, tell me about it."

Pearl began his talk slowly and carefully. "Most bad golfers don't understand that there is a connection between the parts of their golf game. They don't understand that there is a connection between they way they practice, the way they think, the way they play, and the way they score. In other words, they don't make any progress because they don't see the path that leads them to improvement. They focus more on what they are doing incorrectly than on what they are doing correctly. They go to the range and fire ball after ball without having a plan for getting better mentally and physically. They get frustrated and don't turn to others for help. They lack goals and direction."

"I know a lot of people like that," Buck said.

Pearl continued. "Here's a frequent scenario on golf courses: A golfer who has golfed only a handful of times this season is out on the course, having a horrible game - chili dips, duck hooks, fat shots, thin shots, four-putts, lost balls, the whole thing. He is throwing clubs, swearing, making himself miserable, and making everyone around him miserable. Seen that person? Been that person?"

"Yeah," Buck admitted, somewhat embarrassed.

"Inevitably, at some point in our golfing career, we all will experience bouts of relatively poor play. So why do so many of us golfers constantly make ourselves miserable when we are not attaining the level at which we think we should be achieving?"

Buck shrugged his shoulders.

"It's simple: Most golfers erroneously think that a good score is a result rather than understanding that it is a process. In other words, they want a Coke without putting in the obligatory fifty cents. Do you understand?"

"Yes. I think I do."

"Good. Now that you know that, I want you to keep that in the back of your mind. In the front of your mind, I want you to remember the right way to do things, which I'm going to tell you about now. Buck, the path to improvement runs by everything I've been teaching you in our lessons. Shooting a good golf score doesn't just happen by stepping on the course. It takes hard work. Good golfers understand this. They practice hard on their skills and mental skills, and they take what they learn on the range and apply it on the course. In essence, they *take the drill to the field,* meaning they take what they practice and apply it on the course."

Buck nodded to indicate that he followed Pearl's lesson.

"Being a process rather than a result, great golf requires two constants: practice and patience. I call them Pearl's two Ps of great golf." Pearl explained further, "Let me expound: First of all, by practice I don't mean banging out a couple hundred range balls once a week. That type of practice will only lead to two things: sore muscles and the development of bad swing habits. By practice, I mean going to the range on a regular basis and practicing sound fundamentals. Second, by patience I don't mean the modicum of courtesy you extend by waiting for the overly etiquette-conscious group of four-putters ahead of you to get off the green before you hit to it. By patience, I mean the understanding of the cyclical nature of golf, and the ability to remain calm and focused while pulling yourself out of one of the many tailspins your game will eventually encounter.

"A good start to improving your golf game will find you asking some questions to determine your current status as a golfer, the status you want to have, and the methods you will use to get you to your desired level. You should ask a series of questions related to three basic questions: As a golfer, where are you now? Where do you want to be? How will you get there from here?"

"Can you give me some examples?" Buck asked.

"Sure," Pearl said. "Where are you now? To answer this question, ask yourself some more specific questions. What is my handicap? What is my average score? What are my strengths as a golfer? What are my weaknesses? What do I believe about my abilities? How much time do I currently spend practicing? Answering these questions and any others that pop up will give you a good base for determining your current status as a golfer. If some questions lead to more questions, as is the tendency, that's fine. Let the questions flow. The more questions you ask, the more answers you will eventually uncover."

"Hmm," Buck thought about where he was at as a golfer. He had improved greatly as of late. Just this week, he shot his best ever score, an 86.

Pearl's lesson rolled on. "Where do you want to be?" he asked with conviction. "If your answer to this question is Pebble Beach, reach a little further. Do you want to be in a tournament at Pebble Beach or would you be happy just walking that luscious surf-sprayed turf? What score do you want to shoot? What do you want to accomplish? What is your ultimate golf dream? What are your goals for the upcoming season? What are your long-term goals for your golf game? By asking questions about where you want to be as a golfer, try to get a good feel for your goals and expectations for your performance level. How good do you want to be, and what do you want to accomplish?"

As Pearl spoke, Buck thought about the answers to his questions. He had big goals for his game, and he knew exactly what he wanted to do. He indulged himself in a few seconds of fantasy.

"How will you get there from here?" Pearl asked, jolting Buck out of his daydream. 'This is the hardest part. How can you get from your current level of play to the level you desire? What must happen for you to make the necessary improvements? To find the answers to these questions, try to get a feeling for why you are frustrated by not playing better golf. What is it about your current level of play that bothers you? Is it your competitiveness with others, or is it a personal goal, regardless of how others play? If you are concerned about beating others, the best answer is very simple: Find yourself some worse playing partners. But if you want to get better irrespective of the play of others, you need to figure out what you are willing to do in order to improve. Are there specific strengths you want to develop? Are there any drills you need to practice? How much time do you have to practice? How often will you practice? Most importantly, ask yourself how you will determine improvement and how you will measure progress toward your goals. What measuring stick will you use to determine whether you are meeting your goals? Will you determine your progress by scores, some subjective measure, or wager winnings?"

Buck was beginning to get lost in Pearl's lesson. There was a lot to consider. How was he going to keep track of all these questions he had to answer?

As if on cue, Pearl went to his bag and produced a small, flat, wrapped present. He handed it to Buck. "This might help you keep track of your progress as a golfer."

Buck carefully tore into the package. His present was a small, soft cover notebook with lined pages. On the first few pages, Pearl had written some words next to today's date. The first page read *Where are you now?* Under that, there were a few sections such as *Handicap* and *Average Score* that would help define Buck's current golf game. On the next few pages, Buck read the questions *Where do you want to be?* and *How will you achieve your goals?* Each section was followed by more specific titles designed to give Buck an outline to write a specific golf improvement plan.

Pearl gently interrupted Buck's inspection of his journal. "Once you have the answers to your questions, you will have the basis of a pretty good golf improvement strategy. The only thing left to do is determine whether you want to pay the fifty cents to get the Coke. Know what I'm talking about? Once you determine that you are willing to pay the proper price for improvement, playing better golf is relatively simple. The key is this: If you want to play better, you have to practice better. You have to learn how to take the drill to the field."

"So how can I begin to practice better?" Buck asked.

"I've already taught you a lot of things you can do to improve your practices. The first thing most amateurs should do is to consult a teaching pro. A good pro will not only help you improve your current swing but will also help you develop a consistent, repeatable swing that will hold up on the course and allow you to start shooting some decent scores.

"Once your swing is consistent and repeatable and sends the ball roughly where you want it to go, you should start to focus on the mental aspects of game. In order to play better, you must begin to practice better, and better practice begins with a plan."

"You want me to plan my practices?" Buck sounded surprised.

"That's right. I'm suggesting you should plan your practices. Your plan should include which drills you want to work on and how much time you will devote to swing mechanics vs. the mental aspects of the game. Focus on swing mechanics is fine; however, don't overdo mechanical skills and drills. It is better to do five perfect reps of drill, avoiding fatigue and poor mechanics, than it is to do one hundreds reps incorrectly. If you feel you need to devote a large proportion of your practice to swing mechanics, that is fine too. Just be sure to work on your mental game skills every chance you get. Incorporating your mental game into your swing mechanics practice will help you take the drill to the field."

"Okay, what else?" Buck asked.

"After your plan is in place, you should try to stick to it as best you can. You had a reason for planning practice the way you did. For example, you planned your practice to work on weaknesses, bolster specific strengths, fine-tune fundamentals, and so on, so try to stick with it. If, however, during the course of your practice session you feel it is necessary to change the plan, go ahead and change it. It is better to change a plan than to become overly rigid and irritable about sticking to a plan that has no room for flexibility."

"Mmhmm, anything else?"

Pearl blew out a deep breath. "Basically, you need to remember that there is a progression to things. Focus your practice sessions on the points of your game you want to improve or strengthen. Then have fun playing the game. At some point down the road, when you are ready to practice again, take stock of your game and find some priorities to practice. Then practice those, play some more, and practice again. Keep that cycle going."

"How much practice should I have compared to the numbers of rounds I play?" Buck asked.

"Good question," Pearl commended. "How often you practice will probably depend on the level of golf you are at. Pros and competing amateurs practice several times weekly. Weekend players might practice once every couple of weeks. It's up to you. If you do it right, you'll find a balance between practice and play. Remember, the quality of your practice is more important than the quantity of your practice."

Pearl summed up his lesson. "The key to the Coke lesson is this: If you want a Coke from the caddyshack, you have to pay the price Lou is charging for it. If you want to play your best golf, you have to practice your best golf and be patient – your game will evolve cyclically through periods of breakthroughs and setbacks."

While Pearl hit his tee shot, Buck stood quietly with a pensive expression on his face. He remained this way for so long after Pearl hit his shot that Pearl began to wonder if Buck had understood the lesson. "Something the matter?" he asked as he climbed into the cart.

"No. Not really. I was just thinking. You said the keys to developing a golf game were practice and patience."

"That's right," Pearl agreed.

"Well, I was thinking, Pearl. It really seems like there are three Ps to developing a great golf game: practice, patience, and persistence. I think persistence fits in there too, because you can't just be patient with your golf game, you need to keep working at it."

Pearl was impressed. Buck was right. Persistence is needed to improve over the long-term. "I think you're right, Buck. I'll have to change my lessons from now on to include the third P: Practice, patience, and persistence. That's what it takes."

With that, the student had become the teacher, and Pearl knew that Buck was ready for a lifelong pursuit of excellent golf.

Pearl says to remember these tips to keep improving:

1. Use a portion of practice time to work on the fundamentals: grip, posture, alignment, takeaway, follow-through, etc. If you are unsure of how to do this, some lessons from a good teaching pro might be beneficial.

2. Spend at least fifty percent of your full-swing practice time working on mastery. Mastery involves visualizing sending the ball to its target (being the ball) and performing that action. When practicing mastery, make sure you go through a full pre-shot routine every time you hit the ball.

3. Spend at least fifty percent of your overall practice time working on the short game – 120 yards and in, chipping, sand play, and putting. These shots are where most good scores are won or lost.

4. During practice, create the mindset you want to have on the course. Imagine your regular playing partners around you. Visualize the holes you play on most frequently. See, hear, smell, and taste the elements you experience when on the course. If there is a particular problem with your golf game, work on it during practice. Master that problem in your mind by conquering it in practice, then take that sense of mastery and confidence to the course.

5. Focus only on positive thoughts. By positive thoughts, I don't mean that you can't work on weaknesses in your game. By positive thoughts I mean this: Don't think in terms of negatives (e.g. Don't hit it in the water. I hope I don't slice. I keep lifting my head.). Think in terms of positives (e.g. Hit it to the flag. Hit it down the middle with a slight draw. Keep my head down.). Remember, the unconscious mind does not register the word *not*. It only understands positive statements.

By thinking "Do not hit it in the water," your unconscious mind will actually send your body the message, "Do hit it in the water." Also, if your shot does not turn out the way you wanted, refocus on the movements your body should make in the proper swing. Forget about analyzing every little fault. Leave that to your sessions with your teaching pro. Finally, forget the bad shots. Remember only the good ones, and let the feeling of hitting a good shot create confidence in your game.

6. Set goals for yourself to achieve during practice to make practice challenging and fun. For example, shoot for a certain percent of shots to fall within a given distance from a target. Sink a certain number of putts in a row before moving to a new distance or drill. Challenge a friend to a putting or a chipping contest, closest to the hole wins.

7. Always keep in mind that you will play like you practice. In golf, this may not happen every time; golf is just too unpredictable a sport for this to happen. But overall, your game will progress according to how well you practice. If you want to improve an element of your game, practice it.

Be patient and persistent with your progress. Don't expect too much too soon. In fact, periodic setbacks are normal. Look for small improvements and be consistent. The improvement will come over time

Chapter 15: Alpha Buck

The younger young man leaned on his club after shanking one of his few remaining Superbucket balls nearly off the right side of the range. He was tired and sore. His hands were raw from swinging furiously at several hundred range balls.

As he stared blankly at ten remaining balls, trying to muster the strength to send those ten balls to widely various points on the range, he noticed the rhythmic clicks of well struck balls from just behind him. He turned to see a slightly older young man standing in perfect follow through position, watching the flight of his ball.

For lack of energy to swing the club himself, the younger young man stood and watched while the older one proceeded to hit balls in a rhythmic cycle: place a ball, stand behind the ball and look out far into the range, stand next to the ball and look down the range again, take a practice swing, look down the range one more time, waggle the club, swing at the ball, and repeat. Each ball was well struck and landed very near one of the flags placed on the range for target practice.

The younger thought to himself while he watched: What was it about this older one that is so special? Why does he hit the ball so well? As he continued to watch, he thought he realized something: The older young man has a confidence about him. He *grips and rips* the clubs so effortlessly. It's as if he knows exactly what is going to happen with all his shots.

In a short time, the older was done with his small bucket of balls. He picked up his bag and began walking of the range.

"Hey," the younger one called. "How do you hit the ball so well?"

Buck stopped and turned toward him. "It's already in your head, my friend."

"I've heard it's all in my head," the younger one yelled back. "But I don't know what *it* is."

Buck laughed. "You'll know it when you find it," he called as he walked off the range. "I'll tell Pearl to come find you."

"Then will I be able to grip it and rip it like you?" the younger one asked.

Buck stopped in his tracks and reached into his pocket. He unfolded today's scorecard and silently read the scores: Buck, 75; Rich Daddy, 76. He smiled and shook head. "Maybe even better," he said with a laugh. "Maybe even better."

About the Author

Jared M. Wood is a psychologist in Oakland County, MI and a doctoral student in sport psychology at Michigan State University. He specializes in peak performance and athletic performance consulting. By blending knowledge and experience from a wide variety of sources, Jared teaches sport psychology principles to athletes of all skill levels.

Printed in the United States
31035LVS00006B/202-639

9 781420 843453